ANATOMY
OF A BOOK
CONTROVERSY

by WAYNE HOMSTAD

D1056000

Phi Delta Kappa Educational Foundation
Bloomington, Indiana

Cover design by Peg Caudell

Library of Congress Catalog Card Number 95-71074
ISBN 0-87367-482-0
Copyright © 1995 by Wayne Homstad
Bloomington, Indiana

TABLE OF CONTENTS

Part Three
Analysis of the Process

INTRODUCTION

Anatomy of a Book Controversy is a case study that describes one school district's attempt to answer two questions: What should students read? Who should decide what students read? The answers to these questions, how those answers were determined, and an examination of the substance and structure of the answers reveal fundamental principles at work when a community institution attempts to resolve a basic educational problem. Such an examination also reveals why book controversies in particular are difficult to resolve. The book that was at the heart of this controversy is *Go Ask Alice*.

About *Go Ask Alice*

According to the publisher, Avon Flare Books, the manuscript of *Go Ask Alice*, published in 1971, was based on the actual diary of a 15-year-old drug user. A primary theme of the girl's diary is her sense of being lost in a world that seems to make sense to everyone else. According to the editors, the title of the book is related both to Lewis Carroll's *Alice in Wonderland* and to a song called "White Rabbit," by Grace Slick, both of which deal with alienation.

The writer and central figure of the diary is the daughter of a middle-class family. Her father is a college professor. She reports in her diary that she likes the members of her family and that she is especially fond of her grandparents. She writes about typical

1

teenage fears: being too fat, not being liked, failing in school, and not being attractive to boys.

The girl reports that her involvement with drugs began accidentally when she attended a party at which Coca Cola was spiked with LSD. After this initial experience, she reports, she consumed a variety of drugs, among them diet pills, tranquilizers, marijuana, LSD, and heroin. The diarist's attitude toward drugs is negative. She recounts "bad trips" and sexual abuse as a result of her drug habit.

During the course of the book, the author runs away from home two times. In both cases, she endures hardships but is welcomed back when she returns home. As the novel ends, the girl has just been released from a mental institution, having been admitted as a result of a "flashback" drug episode in which she tried to harm herself. On her release from the institution, she ends her diary because she feels that she no longer needs to write in it. In an epilogue to the story, the editors reveal that the writer died of an overdose three weeks after the last entry in her diary.

Greenlaw (1975) suggested that this book is an effective means for teaching about the hazards of drug use. However, Nilsen (1979) criticized the authenticity of the book, claiming that it was not the diary of a young girl but a piece of fiction written by Beatrice Sparks. Nilsen also contended that it is impossible to assess the authenticity of the book because the diary purportedly used to format the plot is locked in the publisher's vault.

Nearly a decade later, Rumsey (1985) suggested that by reading *Go Ask Alice*, students might benefit from vicariously experiencing the diarist's unsuccessful efforts to deal with her complex environment. It was Rumsey's contention that the plot of the book is similar to a morality play. The protagonist attempts to do the right things, but the antagonists thwart her efforts. Rumsey suggested that this morality play is acted out in schools every day.

Although a number of similar claims have been made about the educational merits of *Go Ask Alice*, the book's use in schools has been frequently protested. Burress (1984) reported that in his survey of 30 protests made about the novel, 16 ended with some form of censorship. Even Rumsey (1985) reported that three often-cited reasons for exclusion of the book are its inclusion of obscene language, discussion of drugs, and depiction of sexual violence.

It is now generally conceded that *Go Ask Alice* is a novel, not an actual diary. Its basis may or may not be a real diary, but the situations and attitudes depicted are true-to-life if not actually true. Whether or not it is a useful teaching tool is still open to debate.

The Nature of Book Controversies

Book controversies present two types of problems for school districts. First is the curriculum problem, which is an issue of content. Someone objects to the content of a reading. But the objection itself also raises an issue of process, which is the second type of problem. When an objection to some aspect of a book's content is voiced, the school district must face the problem of processing that objection. Whoever becomes responsible for processing the controversy becomes obligated to react to the curricular issue, or substance of the complaint, and to ensure that the complaint is processed according to the laws and policies that govern the district. Thus, in the context of this study, I define the two halves of a book controversy as *substantial*, related to the contents of the material, and *procedural*, related to the methods used for processing the objection.

Processing an objection to a book and resolving a controversy are complicated tasks because achieving a satisfactory resolution involves dealing with a number of political units both inside and outside the school and the district. Internal political units include board of education members, administrators, and teachers who want to have a share in the resolution. Outside the school other groups, such as church committees and political groups, want to achieve a resolution consistent with their philosophies. Consequently, in processing a book controversy, school district leaders may find themselves at odds with other school personnel, as well as with members of the community.

Furthermore, such controversies may cause school officials to go beyond simply resolving the "problem" of the book protest. The process of responding to the controversy may cause school officials to re-examine policies and philosophies that affect curricular content and administrative processes on a larger scale.

By examining how a school district handles a book controversy in terms of substance, process, and policy reform, a researcher can observe the political and philosophical infrastructures that support education. Observation of the infrastructure in a time of stress over a book controversy also offers insights about institutional values. Therefore, *manifest policies*, which are stated and public, and *latent policies*, which are unstated but often guide the actions of members of the institution, are important to understand because they help to frame a holistic description not simply of a single action, but rather of a community institution at work.

One particularly valuable perspective for viewing and evaluating a controversy can be derived from examining the arguments made by key players in the controversy. And the examination of such arguments can reveal essential information about the importance of the arguments to the persons presenting them.

Therefore, in constructing *Anatomy of a Book Controversy*, I have aimed toward four objectives:

- To describe the controversy that resulted from a middle school teacher's assignment of the novel, *Go Ask Alice*;
- To examine the processes used by district officials to resolve this controversy and to discuss what those processes reveal about how schools solve controversies in general;
- To discuss the power of image-based thinking and how that type of thinking interfered with the resolution of this book controversy; and
- To discuss the broader implications of image-based thinking in developing solutions to educational problems.

Anatomy of a Book Controversy and Its Precedents

Anatomy of a Book Controversy traces themes developed by other writers. Viewing a school district as an institutional entity is a sociological act discussed by Besag and Nelson (1984). Developing a holistic sense of an issue is practiced by both Peshkin (1986) and Moffet (1988). Examining the substance of a book controversy is an extension of the work done by Burress (1984) and Donelson (1987). However, and perhaps most important, describing how a problem was solved by a school district may be a helpful extension of the concepts developed by Tyack (1974) and Coons and Sugarman (1978), who advocated solving potential or anticipated problems through policy reform.

A general theme of *Anatomy of a Book Controversy* is that understanding institutional problems involves both definition and solution. If the definition of a problem is incomplete, then its solution is likely to be inadequate. If the problem is defined adequately but the solution is limited, then it is likely that the problem will recur.

School districts are social institutions that include many people with many institutional roles. Thus the problems that develop must be evaluated from many different perspectives. The book controversy discussed in this volume is first described chronologically and then from the perspectives of the four individuals most involved in the controversy: the parent, the superintendent, the teacher, and the director. Each perspective is unique and so provides a singular interpretation of the controversy.

Procedures of the Study

The primary data for this study were collected through personal interviews of the people connected to the controversy. Their names have been changed in this book to protect their privacy. All of the individuals who were interviewed were cooperative and thoughtful in answering my questions. Their role in the development of the study was to help make the description of the controversy as complete as possible. I have treated their input objectively, as any assessment on my part of wrong-doing by any participant in this controversy would be outside the limits of the data and beyond the scope of this study.

All of the 23 people I interviewed had some direct connection to the controversy. Some had attended the school board meeting at which the protest was made. Some served on committees that dealt with the controversy. Some were active in organizing group reactions to the process by which the controversy was handled. Four of those interviewed had key roles in the controversy. These four — the parent who protested the book, the substitute teacher who assigned the book, the superintendent of schools, and the director of instructional services — were interviewed twice.

Of these 23 people, ten were female and eight were classroom English teachers. One person taught at the elementary level. Three taught at the middle school level, and four taught at the high school level. A librarian from each level also was interviewed. Two classroom specialists, two members of the school board, and five administrators were interviewed. With the exception of the substitute teacher who assigned *Go Ask Alice*, all of those interviewed had been employees of the school district for more than five years, and most had been employed by the district for more than 12 years.

Written sources of information included the superintendent's file on the controversy, committee reports, and newspaper accounts. The superintendent's file, considered the official school district record of the controversy, was made available; it included letters, memos, and copies of the committee reports.

The most important committee report came from the Supplementary Materials Review Committee. It was the responsibility of this committee to evaluate the novel and its usefulness in the middle school curriculum. Another significant report came from the Policy Review Committee. The Policy Review Committee evaluated, revised, and updated policies that were used in arriving at a resolution to the book controversy.

Newspaper accounts of the controversy were easy to gather. Twice during the span of the controversy the topic was treated as front-page news. At other times, the reporting of the controversy was left to small articles, editorials, and letters to the editor. During the interview sessions, some subjects also reported hearing about the controversy in radio news reports.

I collected data from committee reports by attending meetings and asking committee personnel to provide duplicate copies of their work. The superintendent's file was made available for duplication. Some of the newspaper reports were obtained by contacting the newspaper directly, and some were obtained as clippings kept by committees interested in the controversy.

The most elaborate means of collecting data was the interview process. Each interview began with basic census questions, such as name, age, experience in the school district, and current position. Three general questions then guided the interview after the census questions: What happened? What should have happened? How did what happened affect the school district? Finally, all of the respondents were asked to make any additional comments that they felt might be important to understanding the controversy.

The interviews were recorded using a small tape recorder, and I took notes during the interviews. After each interview, I annotated the handwritten notes. Later, a stenographer's tape recorder was used to review the audio tape and further annotate the notes. Finally, the taped interviews were given to a secretary who transcribed them.

As mentioned earlier, four key individuals were interviewed twice. The primary purpose of the second interview was to review and clarify information. Two secondary goals also were achieved. First, the respondents were given a chance to rephrase or restate their previous positions on the controversy. Second, because these individuals were to be singled out in the report, it gave me the opportunity to explain how I was going to use the information.

These second interviews also were audio-taped, and I developed annotated notes, but the tapes were not transcribed for three reasons: 1) the information was consistent with the first interviews, 2) a mechanical problem affected the quality of two of the recordings, and 3) the secretary was unavailable for transcription.

A problem involving respondents who were recorded deserves comment. Even though the tape recorder was small and set off to one side, its presence seemed intrusive. I found that when the interview reached a conclusion and the tape recorder had been shut off, many respondents relaxed and shared more information. Thus I found it valuable to be alert for information that came after the tape recorder was no longer a factor in the conversation.

Hours of taped interviews, more than 300 pages of typed transcripts, notebooks of rough notes, and volumes of reading materials made it difficult to isolate the most significant themes and difficult to find the most important details. Therefore, I found it most useful to organize the data into the general categories that were used during the interviews:

What happened?
What should have happened?
How did what happened affect the school district?

Examining the data about what happened provided a chronological description of the controversy. Newspaper reports and documents from the superintendent's file helped complete that basic outline. From the chronological outline, I was able to determine which events were more significant than others and which people had the most significant roles in those events. Data from the interview transcripts expanded the chronological description of the controversy.

"What should have happened?" is not an objective question; consequently, those answers were more difficult to organize. However, by comparing the interview responses to information developed in the chronological description, I found that basic themes emerged. These basic themes, in turn, developed into answers to the final question, "How did what happened affect the school district?"

Limitations of This Study

This analysis, like most such studies, has been written with the luxury of hindsight that the participants in the midst of the controversy did not enjoy. Historical perspective allows a researcher to evaluate the recollected thoughts and actions of individuals and to connect their reflective evaluations to the facts of the controversy. Of course, many of those connections that can be made at a distance and by a detached observer were impossible for the individuals embroiled in the immediacy of the controversy to make.

In addition, the magnification and examination for research purposes of one event (or sequence of events) in a person's life must necessarily constrain the comments and opinions of the researcher. Isolating one event and focusing on it can mislead readers (and the researcher), who may be inclined to forget that for the duration of this controversy the participants were not static characters in a drama. Therefore, it is helpful to remember that before, during, and after the controversy, the participants functioned simultaneously as parents, teachers, administrators, and so on.

This study also is bounded by time limits. The controversy began on 5 May 1987. Officially, it was resolved on 15 June 1987. However, limiting the research to such a short period in a school district's history would increase the chances that important effects of the controversy might be overlooked. It was not until December 1989, for example, that the report of the Policy Review Committee was presented to the board of education. Therefore, a more reasonable research time frame is the period from 5 May 1987 to 15 December 1989.

Ultimately this report is an abstraction. The actions and thoughts of the participants — parent, teacher, superintendent, director — represent points of view in the controversy. Because of commitments of anonymity made to the interviewees, the names and places recorded in this study are fictitious. However, the events, actions, and recorded words of the players are real.

I wish to acknowledge two individuals who have contributed to the completion of this book. Thanks to the patient and careful mentoring of Professor Richard Western of the University of Wisconsin-Milwaukee, I have found education to be a rewarding and lifelong pursuit. And thanks to the constant encouragement of Donovan Walling, I have continued to grow in my understanding of the art of writing.

PART ONE
The Controversy

CHAPTER ONE

DEVELOPMENT OF THE CONTROVERSY

BOOK SHELVED: Middle Schools Can't Go Ask Alice Anymore

(By Bob Brown, *Newport Press*, 6 May 1987, page 1.)

"Last night was the worst night of my ___, rotten, stinky, dreary life." (Quote from *Go Ask Alice*)

Superintendent of Schools, Dr. G. Roberts has ordered a book taken off the approved reading list in the public school district's three middle schools because it contains "words I don't feel are appropriate."

The book, *Go Ask Alice*, which is based on an actual diary of the an anonymous teenage drug user, was brought to the attention of Roberts and the Newport Board of Education in a dramatic way during the board's Community Input Session Tuesday night.

John Andrews, 2100 N. Ninth St., a Washington High School teacher, read excerpts from the book, jolting the more than 100 persons attending the public meeting.

"I'm very sorry if you found that offensive, but I do," Andrews said. "If I had said I found it offensive you might have thought they were words like 'hell' or something like that. You can see they're not."

Andrews said the book is one of a group of books from which seventh-graders at Lincoln Middle School must select their required language arts reading.

"If students used that language in the halls of the middle school or the high school, they would be suspended," Andrews said.

Andrews, who said the message of the book was good but the profanity not, said he didn't think those words should be read or spoken, adding that he was "very concerned" that such a book would be on a required reading list.

Roberts thanked Andrews for bringing the book to his attention, and the superintendent told *The Press* after the meeting that "the book would be pulled."

"I talked with David Walker (coordinator of reading and language arts) and Martin Olson (director of instructional services), and I told them that if a list is an approved list, a better job should be done of reviewing the books on such a list."

William Rohr, president of the board, said he was "surprised, shocked, dismayed and disappointed" that a book with that profanity was in the middle schools.

"I was embarrassed as a board member that we have a book on a reading list with that kind of language," Rohr said. "Frankly, that type of book shouldn't be on the shelves of a library, especially at that level."

Rohr said that he was concerned with what committee or group of educators had approved the book, which he said was "out of step" with the Newport community.

Roberts said he felt that some people might view his action in pulling the book a form of censorship, but he added that the district has a policy dealing with complaints about reading materials in the district.

Olson said if someone has a complaint about a particular book, they have the option of selecting another book from the approved list.

By board policy, complaints are made by contacting the building principal and filling out a form which is turned in to the principal, who then reviews the book with the librarian and at least three teachers.

A report is then given to the complaining person, and if that response is deemed insufficient, the complaint goes to Olson for consideration.

Olson said the complaint could, according to school board policy, eventually reach the Board of Education's Professional, Personnel and Instruction Committee.

This newspaper report is the first written description of an event that became the *"Go Ask Alice* Controversy." The newspaper report is important for three reasons. First, its front-page banner headline alerted readers that a book protest was being made in one of the public schools. Second, it gave three of the four key players in the controversy an opportunity to express opinions. Third, it provides a written record against which further discussion of the controversy can be examined.

As reported by the *Newport Press*, the controversy surrounding the use of *Go Ask Alice* began at an open-forum school board meeting on 5 May 1987. But a true chronology of the controversy must begin somewhat earlier, with the assignment of the book as a student reading.

The Assignment of *Go Ask Alice*

Go Ask Alice was assigned to a seventh-grade reading class at Lincoln Middle School by a long-term substitute teacher. Mrs. Hansen, the substitute, had replaced the regular classroom teacher, who was on maternity leave. The assignment was made on Monday, May 4. Lesson plans for the assignment had been handed in to the principal during the previous week.

Hansen later stated three reasons for using *Go Ask Alice*. First, she recognized that the reading level of this group of students was higher than average. Second, she reported that she was following the advice of the regular classroom teacher, who recommended using the book in part because there were sufficient copies so that each student could use one. Thus the third reason was simply practical availability.

Hansen also cited five goals that could be accomplished by using *Go Ask Alice*. First, she had been told that the students in this class read a novel a week, and she did not want to re-use any novel that had already been read as the students continued that pace. Second, the students were going to study the diary format as used in literature and to compare the diary format to other literary formats that they already had encountered. Third, students were supposed to apply skills in analyzing major and minor characters that they had learned from studying previous novels. Fourth, the teacher wanted to provide an opportunity for students to investigate a socially relevant topic. The relevant social topics to be discussed during their reading of *Go Ask Alice* were drug use and the effects of peer pressure. The fifth goal was "to provide students with thinking skill experiences using information needed to make sound decisions."

A Chronology of the Protest

Development of the Protest: May 4. On Monday, May 4, copies of *Go Ask Alice* were distributed to the students. Later that day, one of the students was reading the novel while driving with her father to the airport to meet her mother. On the way to the airport, she began to tell her father about the contents of *Go Ask Alice.*

Community Input Session: May 5. The board of education for the Newport Area School District holds four Community Input Sessions each year. The purpose of these sessions is to allow citizens to address the board of education on issues of their choice outside the more constraining structure of the formal monthly board meetings. The first citizen to address the board at this Tuesday evening session was John Andrews, the parent of the student who had been reading *Go Ask Alice* on the way to the airport. While there are no detailed, official records of Andrew's protest, interviews with some of the persons who were present at the input session indicate that the description of events as reported by Brown in the newspaper account is accurate. In stating his protest to *Go Ask Alice*, Andrews read excerpts from the novel. Brown did not quote Andrews' reading in full, but one of the lines read by Andrews was: "Last night was the worst night of my shitty, rotten, stinky, dreary, fucked up life."

Brown's newspaper report states that the superintendent of schools responded to the parent by thanking him for bringing the matter to his attention. But more than that occurred. Several individuals who attended the meeting reported that the superintendent also said, "The book is gone," which they took to mean that use of the book would be discontinued immediately. The superintendent remembered saying, "That book will not be read. . . . It will be off the shelf tomorrow." Thus, by the end of the meeting, the protest had been heard and action had been taken regarding the use of the book. The superintendent had decided then and there to discontinue the novel's use.

Immediate Reactions to the Protest: May 6. Reporters from two local radio stations also had attended the Community Input Session. Their reports were broadcast early the next morning, Wednesday. Hansen, the teacher who assigned the book, was driving to work that morning when she heard a news report of the protest on her car radio. She described her arrival at Lincoln Middle School with the following words:

> I got to school and people came running into my room saying, "If any newspaper people, or if any — or if a helicopter — whatever, lands out in the field and they want to talk to you, tell them you have no comment." . . . I couldn't even tell you who it was, but that's what they said. Just saying, "no comment" and "collect the books immediately" . . . because the directive had come down from the board of education that they had to be turned in.

No one remembers who actually ordered the collection of the books; no written records document this action. Sometime early in the morning of May 6, the superintendent did call the principals of the district's three middle schools and asked them to discontinue the use of *Go Ask Alice* until an investigation could be completed. According to sources in the other two middle schools, the request was carried out. But apparently, the request was handled most immediately at Lincoln Middle School. According to Hansen and the school librarian, the students were asked by the principal to turn in the books. If the books were not at school, the students were sent home to get them or asked to have a parent deliver the books to school. The librarian commented:

They [unidentified personnel] came here and made the kids go to their lockers and remove them [copies of *Go Ask Alice*] physically in a box the next day. . . . They didn't even come during the reading class. So first, they had to find these kids that were scattered all over the place, and then — I mean, they couldn't have made it any more dramatic unless they had lit a fire on the front steps of the school [laughs].

As reported by Brown in the *Newport Press*, the superintendent met with Olson, the director of instructional services (later referred to simply as the director), and Walker, the coordinator of language arts and reading (the coordinator), on the morning of May 6. Brown quoted the superintendent as saying, "I told them that if a list is an approved list, a better job should be done of reviewing the books on such a list."

The Letters and Other Reactions: May 8-14. Subsequently, the superintendent began to receive letters from community people. The first letter, dated May 8, was from the parent of another student at Lincoln Middle School who was unhappy with the way in which the protest was made and with the way in which the superintendent had handled the matter. In her letter, this parent supported the use of *Go Ask Alice* as a supplementary text. The superintendent responded on May 12 with a letter in which he accepted responsibility for removing the book from the class.

Also among the first letters was one from Eunice Edgar, executive director of the American Civil Liberties Union of Wisconsin Foundation. Edgar's letter requested information about the protest. The letter was immediately referred to the board of education's attorney. With the receipt of the Edgar letter, the controversy had taken on another issue — the potential for legal intervention. Thus another of the district's specialists, a lawyer, had been pulled into the controversy.

Other comments about the controversy appeared in the editorial section of the local newspaper. In a "letters to the editor" column, one unnamed writer supported the use of the book as a result of personal experiences with drugs.

A student from the seventh-grade reading class at Lincoln Middle School also wrote a letter of protest to the board of education. The student argued that even though foul language appeared in the book, she was aware of the terms, had seen them written and heard them spoken, before she read *Go Ask Alice*. The student knew that such "language is never right"; but she felt that the language made the characters more believable. In another part of her letter, the student wanted to know why a book became unacceptable because one person objected to it.

Opposition to the superintendent's directive to remove the book also began to develop among personnel in the school district. A group of librarians and media specialists, the Media Committee, sent a letter to the superintendent that was critical of this action:

> We believe the removal of the book was unwarranted, premature, and contraindicated by the board policy of the Newport Area School District. To say the least, the events which occurred at the public input session were confusing and shocking. The *Newport Press* quoted you as saying that you felt some people might view your action of pulling this book as a form of censorship, but you added that the district has a policy dealing with complaints about reading materials. You are correct on both accounts. We do view your action as an act of censorship and there is a board policy dealing with challenged materials. . . . We respectfully request that *Go Ask Alice* be returned to the middle schools immediately, *pending a review of the material through the adopted policy, if a written complaint is filed as indicated in that policy.*

Later, in an undated petition that was forwarded to the superintendent before the end of the school year, 37 faculty members from Lincoln Middle School asked that *Go Ask Alice* be returned to the library.

Reactions continued for several weeks after the main reaction period that immediately followed the protest. For example, on June 4 the superintendent received a letter from the police liaison officer at Lincoln Middle School. The main point of the letter was that the book could be used as a tool to show the destructive nature of drugs. The police officer wrote, "I see *Go Ask Alice* as a catalyst to encourage discussion about some very serious and far reaching problems that our community faces."

In many ways, two distinct camps began to form very quickly after the protest. One comprised those who sympathized with the protesting parent and wanted to see the book's use discontinued or, more extreme, wanted to see the book completely removed from schools. The other camp comprised individuals who questioned the legitimacy of the superintendent's unilateral decision to remove the book and urged a more considered response. Therein lay much of the controversy. Which camp would prevail? Or could a compromise position be found?

CHAPTER TWO

PROCESSING THE CONTROVERSY

On the day after the Community Input Session, the superintendent met with the director and the coordinator. The superintendent assigned responsibility for handling the controversy to the director. The director then wrote a memo to the middle school principals that stated the steps that already had been taken to resolve the controversy. He wrote in part:

> We are reviewing it [*Go Ask Alice*] per policy 6144, page 3. Dr. Roberts [the superintendent] has directed that the book not be used for instruction in the interim. . . . This is not a complaint about a library book under policy 6163.1. The book need not be removed from the library if it is part of the collection.

Policy 6144 applies to the use of supplementary books. Policy 6163 applies to library books.

This memo to the middle school principals is significant for three reasons. First, the director limited the scope of the parent protest to supplemental texts. This meant that the controversy about the novel's use had nothing to do with regular textbooks or with books that compose the library collection. The effect of this limitation was to allow the librarians to place the book back on the library shelves for general circulation.

Second, by defining the controversy in terms of Policy 6144, the director was highlighting a set of procedures that differ from those spelled out in Policy 6163. Thus the director identified a specific method for evaluating the use of the book.

Third, the decision to apply only Policy 6144 — thereby restoring the book to the libraries — also blunted the criticism of the superintendent's actions by the Media Committee and by the petitioners from Lincoln Middle School, both of whom cited Board Policy 6163 as the source of correct procedures for resolving the controversy.

It is important to note that, from this point onward in the processing of the controversy, the resolution was being orchestrated by the director, not the superintendent. More important, the resolution was being framed within board policies, rather than by the direction of the superintendent, whose order to remove the book had been interpreted by some observers to be contrary to board policy.

The Director's Procedures

The director's involvement was crucial from early in the controversy. For example, memos dated May 14 show that the director of instructional services and the coordinator of language arts and reading had already begun to develop a plan for evaluating reading lists. Their discussion is summarized best in the memo written by the coordinator:

> [T]he issue of appropriate level (readability and/or maturity) is to some extent peripheral. The central issue is one of control. How much control over book selection for supplementary materials should teachers and individual buildings have? How should they exercise that control? Simply generating a list [of supplemental texts for each level] is of little value if no control is exerted to ensure that those books listed are appropriate (again, by whose judgment?) for the intended students. The suggestion of a building-level review committee is moved by a notion that such a committee might cause teachers and principals to become more aware of the supplementary materials, thus tightening their own

control of the situation — without direct interference from the central office.

At the director's instruction, the coordinator wrote a memo on May 27 to the parent who had protested the use of the book. The coordinator informed the parent about the formation of a four-member review committee, the date on which the book would be reviewed, the policy that governed the review process, and the options open to the parent if he chose to present information to the committee. This review committee was scheduled to meet on June 15.

In the meantime, in a memo dated June 5 the director asked the principal of Lincoln Middle School to provide information regarding the intended use of *Go Ask Alice* in terms of purpose, issues to be discussed, assignments, classroom activities, and reasons for the selection of the novel. The director also asked for information about how the assignment was presented to the students, specifically:

> Were students advised that the book might be controversial or objectionable to some persons? Were students offered the opportunity to select or use materials other than the book? If so, how?

The director concluded this memo by announcing that the complaint about *Go Ask Alice* would be reviewed in his office at 1:30 p.m. on June 15 and stating, "You and/or the teacher, of course, may attend the review, if you wish."

The School's Report

The information requested by the director was provided in a report dated June 9 from the Lincoln Middle School principal and the reading consultant. The substitute teacher assisted in writing the report, which answered each of the questions posed in the director's memo. Among the 10 enumerated answers in this document, the following are the most revealing:

2. The book was planned to be used as "supplementary" reading to our basal reading series. Mr. D. Walker, Reading and Language Arts Coordinator, had recently encouraged teachers to "depart" from the basal so students' reading could be broadened and/or enriched. Other major purposes for the choice of this book were to (a) study another writing style and compare it to others studied previously; (b) understand characterization and examine various elements that led to a character change; (c) provide opportunities to investigate a relevant topic, hoping to provide suitable alternatives and choice as it relates to the harmful effects of peer pressure and drug/chemical abuse; and, (d) provide students with thinking skill experiences using information needed to make sound decisions. . . .

5. The book was distributed to the reading class on Tuesday, May 5, 1987. The class was, after a brief introduction, given an assignment to read to page 94 prior to Friday, May 8. BEFORE the class had any discussion or activities, the book was ordered removed from the Reading Center collection. We immediately upon the instructions of Superintendent of Schools, Dr. George Roberts, collected all copies of *Go Ask Alice* from the students.

6. The book was shelved BEFORE ANY CLASS DISCUSSIONS WERE HELD.

7. The students were aware that the book was about a young girl's involvement with drugs and how it affected her life.

8. We believe students were aware of the opportunity to select or use materials other than the book. The complainant's daughter had already been given an opportunity to make an alternate selection on a previous occasion.

Point number 8 is especially important because it states for the first time that the parent had previously objected to a book that had been assigned to his daughter's reading class earlier in the school year. The protest he voiced at the Community Input Session was his second. According to the teacher, the parent had earlier protested the assigned reading of the novel, *The Disappearance*, and, as in the *Go Ask Alice* protest, the issue was profanity.

24

Before she helped the reading consultant write the report detailing the proposed use of *Go Ask Alice*, the teacher consulted an attorney. The attorney advised the teacher to help the reading consultant complete the document, but he also advised the teacher to develop her own document detailing her role in assigning the novel and her reasons for making the assignment.

At the same time that he was collecting information about the use of the novel, the director also was concerned with legal implications of the controversy. On June 8 he wrote a letter to the board of education's attorney, asking if he was correct in his interpretation of Policy 6144. Additionally, he specifically asked about the power of the Supplementary Materials Review Committee's findings. In short, was he obligated to follow the findings of the committee or merely to consider them as he made a decision regarding the book?

Records indicate that the board's attorney was active in helping to resolve the controversy. According to handwritten notes, a telephone conference that included the attorney, the director, and the coordinator occurred at 9:35 a.m. on June 12. The conference centered on the agenda for the review committee meeting, which was scheduled for three days later on June 15. The attorney followed up the telephone conference by writing a summary of the discussion and sending along a proposed agenda. This was done on the same day as the conference call. The agenda proposed by the attorney became the guide for the meeting of the review committee. Also on June 12, the attorney forwarded the information requested by the ACLU of Wisconsin Foundation.

CHAPTER THREE

THE OFFICIAL RESOLUTION

The Supplementary Materials Review Committee met on June 15. Although there are no records that describe the formation of the committee, the group was organized specifically to review the use of *Go Ask Alice*. Apparently the committee had been formed before May 27. The first document that mentions the committee's work is a memo from the coordinator to committee members, advising them that the proposed date of the committee meeting had been changed to June 15. The memo was sent to the citywide chairman of the Language Arts Department, a middle school reading consultant, and the chairman of the Elementary Language Arts Department.

The agenda for the committee contained eight items. Routine business, such as introducing the committee members, selecting a recorder, reviewing the procedures, and explaining the purpose of the meeting, constituted the first two items on the agenda. Items 3 and 4 were marked for presentation of the complaint by the parent and a discussion of the book's use by someone from within the school district. Under item 5, the committee would consider two questions:

- Was the book used appropriately in light of the policy?
- Should the book continue to be used?

Under item 6 a committee report would be developed, and under item 7, the complainant would be given a preliminary response from the committee. Item 8 was adjournment.

The official record of the proceedings was written by the coordinator. He noted that 13 people attended the meeting. The four "official" committee members were present, and seven people in attendance were described as "interested participants." The category of "interested participants" included several individuals from Lincoln Middle School: the substitute teacher, the principal, the librarian, and the reading consultant. Others in this category were the superintendent and a librarian from another middle school. Andrews, the parent who made the complaint, was accompanied by his wife.

The official record of the meeting was not a verbatim transcript, but rather a summary of statements made. This record indicates that the committee meeting was informal, not marked by adherence to parliamentary procedure or to the order of items listed on the agenda. Comments made during the deliberations seem often to have been random. For example, in his record, the coordinator listed 45 "agenda responses." The first five responses followed the agenda as established by the attorney. Points 6 and 7 show that the order established in the agenda was amended. At point 6, the principal of Lincoln Middle School requested that the committee's minutes show that the novel was collected as directed by the superintendent. After this request was granted, the substitute teacher began to explain her reasons for using *Go Ask Alice*. Copies of the letter that she drafted after consulting with her attorney were distributed to the committee, and she reviewed her arguments made in the letter. The teacher's testimony was followed by that of the reading consultant.

After the presentations of the teacher and the reading consultant, committee members asked questions. Committee members wanted to know how alternative reading assignments were given and how students were made aware that alternative reading assignments were available. The teacher said that after she summarized the story line for the students, she told them that they could choose a different novel if they wished. The teacher told the committee that she did not warn the students that the contents of the book might be objectionable.

At this point the principal added that the school policy regarding alternative assignments was verbal; it did not exist in written form. Then the director commented that there was no formal policy regarding alternative reading assignments in the school district.

The parent commented that the assignment given to his daughter as an alternative to reading *The Disappearance* had been acceptable. However, in the case of *Go Ask Alice*, his concern became more general and encompassed the other children in the classroom. He felt that most students would not discuss assigned readings with their parents if the students felt that the parents would find the readings objectionable.

The mother argued that the alternative assignment policy had not been communicated clearly. She questioned the authenticity of the book as a diary. She also objected to the explicit descriptions of sexual acts. The father cited material from 21 different pages of the book as having objectionable language.

After the parents addressed the committee, the discussion became general. One of the committee members reported about her daughter's personal experience with *Go Ask Alice*. This same committee member mentioned that one of the themes in the book is lack of communication between parents and children. The mother then commented that she felt the sexual references might arouse students' curiosity and raise questions that the classroom teacher might find difficult to answer. At this point the reading consultant suggested that such questions were probably better handled by a classroom teacher, and he suggested that the discussion focus on the "beautiful things" found in the book.

The mother continued to argue that the book did not give hope or solutions. She felt that the parents should read the book, not the children. The mother's comments were followed by a committee member's comment that the book was "powerful" and its intent is to "turn kids off of drugs."

The parents made two further arguments. First, the father commented that the language in the novel would not be tolerated in the schools or in most homes. Second, the mother suggested that the book was not an accurate depiction of the "drug scene" because the "drug scene" had changed since the book was written.

At this point, the superintendent posed four questions to the committee:

1. Was the book approved as part of the curriculum?
2. How are our supplementary books selected?
3. How are our library books selected?
4. What purpose or purposes do the books serve?

Although these questions seem to be central to understanding book controversies in general, only the first question received much attention from the committee. The director explained the approval process for books to be used as part of the curriculum. His explanation was followed by a comment from a committee member about age-appropriateness of books. This committee member thought that the central question facing the committee was, "At what level [age/grade] do we provide certain information to children?"

Subsequent to these comments, the committee seemed to reach a decision regarding the use of *Go Ask Alice*. Again, the following statements (not verbatim) illustrate the random quality of committee members' comments:

Member 1: The book was used appropriately. . . . It must be clear that alternatives are available.

Member 2: I agree. . . . The book should be used. We can't hide material just because it is objectionable.

Member 3: I don't know that I want the book taught, but it does deal with important issues. Alternatives should be considered, but this book should remain, at least in the meantime.

Director: The book was used appropriately. I am concerned that we have no way to alert parents and students. . . . Such a controversial book may detract from teaching rather than add to it. Some families in the community may object. The book should be in the schools for use with some individuals.

30

During the final phase of the committee meeting, the members attempted to reach consensus. They all agreed that the book had been used appropriately. The final positions adopted by the committee are summarized in these two statements from the coordinator's minutes:

1. The book may be used in the future. Alternatives should be provided.

2. Three members of the committee felt that the book might be used with the class. One committee member did not. The committee decided that a written report would be drafted and reviewed at a later date.

The Preliminary Report

That later written report was titled "Report of Review Committee Regarding a Complaint About the Use of the Book *Go Ask Alice*." The main finding was framed in the following manner:

Section A - Decision

It is the decision of the committee that the book *Go Ask Alice* should continue to be used in the middle schools for educational goals that it suits, provided that students and parents are advised of potentially controversial content and alternate materials can be selected by them.

Section B of the report is titled "Rationale/Reasons." This section includes two important ideas; however, neither idea is a reason or a rationale. First, the committee commented:

The committee is agreed that the book was appropriately used, or would have been appropriately used had the lesson plan developed by Mrs. Hansen been allowed to be carried out.

The committee's intention in using the phrase, "appropriately used," is unclear. The term could refer to the age of the students and the book's appropriateness for that age level. Or the term could be applied to the use of the book in the context of the teacher's lesson. The term also might apply to the teacher's decision that she was the appropriate person to be teaching about the content of the book.

Because the concept of appropriateness was not clearly defined, the committee found it impossible to achieve consensus. The second part of Section B catalogues the votes by the four "official" members of the committee. Two members felt that the book would be appropriate for future use with entire classes. One member felt that the book could not be used with some classes and that an alternative selection would be more appropriate. The fourth member felt that the book should not be used with entire classes, but that it might be appropriate for use with certain individual students. All four members believed that alternative reading assignments must be available and that the availability of alternatives must be communicated to students and parents.

Section C of the report lists the appeal rights of the complainants as described in Policy 6144. This section alerted the parents about the next steps they might take in processing their protest if they were dissatisfied with the findings of the committee.

On June 16, the director sent a memo to the individuals who had served on the committee, thanking them for their participation. Attached to the memo was a copy of the minutes and the preliminary report. The director asked each member to review both documents:

> Please return to me, by June 19, if possible, your written approval or suggestions for change. If there are changes of substance proposed, I will discuss them with all members . . . . For your information, the *Press* has requested information about our meeting. I gave Bob Brown general information, but indicated that the final report was not available pending your review of the attached.

The Final Report

The final report was written by the director and presented to the superintendent on July 1. Much of the information in the final report repeats the contents of the preliminary report. However, the final report differs significantly from the preliminary report in its conclusions about the use of *Go Ask Alice*.

The conclusion reached in the final report is that the novel is *not* appropriate for use as a supplementary text in the middle schools. This decision contradicts the finding of the committee. In the final report, the director explains to the superintendent that he was empowered to contradict the committee and gives his reasons for arriving at such a decision.

First, the director cited Board Policy 6144:

> [T]he review committee shall make its report to the complainant through the Director of Instruction and that, if the complainant is not satisfied with the decision of the committee and Director of Instruction, he may take the matter to the superintendent for further review.

The director's interpretation of this section of the policy was that he had the power to make a decision concerning the book and that the decision reached by the committee was advisory, not obligatory. Therefore, he felt empowered to ignore the committee's decision and develop one of his own.

His decision and its justifications are spelled out in the report as follows:

> I find that the book is not appropriate for use as a supplementary text with middle school reading or language arts classes for three reasons. First, the language and controversial content of the book detract from the prime purposes intended — developing literary appreciation, studying the diary format, and learning about characterization. The need to inform students and parents of potentially objectionable language and content and the fact that some students and parents do find them objectionable *per se* detract from the prime goals of reading instruction.
>
> Second, there are other supplementary materials that will suit the prime instructional goals as well. *Go Ask Alice* is far from being great literature. There are other books with diary

format that will appeal to the middle school age group and other books that will do a better job with characterization and other literary techniques.

Third, there are better media for the secondary purpose for which the book was used, providing opportunities to investigate drug use and abuse. The book is not entirely factual but may appear so. Recent news reports of the deaths of youths from drug abuse would be factual and have the same potential emotional impact. Health education teachers and others do use other media for drug education in the middle schools.

The last paragraphs of the final report informed the superintendent that building committees would be established to review supplementary materials so that instructional goals could be met. It also mentions that some policies need review, specifically Board Policy 6144, which had been crucial to the report.

On July 13 copies of the preliminary report and the final report were sent to the district's principals along with a memo from the director. In his memo, the director advised the principals to note the final paragraphs of his report, in which he called for the development of building committees to review supplementary materials.

After the Final Report: Action and Reaction

On July 13, the director also sent a letter to the parents who had protested the use of the novel. Included with the letter was a copy of the final report. In one sense, the writing of this letter to the parent was the last official act regarding the *Go Ask Alice* controversy. However, at this point many aspects of the controversy had not been settled, and the long-term effects were only beginning to develop.

In the July 15 *Newport Press,* columnist Marion Smith's article carried the headline, "Let Them Read the Book." Smith's column opened by paraphrasing the superintendent's and the school board president's statements to the press after the Community Input Session of May 5. For example, on May 5 the board president was quoted as saying, "Frankly, I am shocked, dismayed, and disappointed . . ." Smith's paraphrase elaborates, attributing the following to the president:

> And, frankly, I'm surprised, to say nothing of shocked, dismayed, and disappointed that these critics didn't at least read the book before they condemned it on the basis of bad language.

Smith then argued that, although the plot of the novel depicted unsavory events, the fiction still had authenticity and authority. Smith wrote:

> It's about a youngster who is sucked into the horrifying world of drug addicts and drug addiction — and who doesn't come out of it alive. The language in *Go Ask Alice* is not language that "Alice" herself would be using in the halls of her high school. But it IS language that a girl whose drug use had separated her from her family's standards and from her own fragile sense of self, a girl whose associations had narrowed to pushers and addicts seems likely to have used — in her diary, in her own private desperate thoughts.

Smith closed her column with an additional warning. She cautioned readers to remember that there was another lesson that the *Go Ask Alice* controversy could teach. The additional lesson was about censorship. Smith wrote:

> [I]t's important that the challenge to carefully and legitimately selected books be met thoughtfully — and with courage. Otherwise, folks, what we'll be teaching our kids is not how to live and learn in a democracy, but how censorship weakens a democracy. And that would be a lesson in irony.

On July 17, a headline in the *Newport Press* read, "*Go Ask Alice* Back in the Library but Out of Classroom." This article, written by Brown, who had covered the controversy since it began, described the decision reached by the director as documented in the final report. Reported Brown:

The controversial book, *Go Ask Alice*, will be back on the library shelves at the three Newport Area School District middle schools this fall, but the book will not be used as supplemental reading in language arts classes at the schools. That decision has been reached by Dr. Martin Olson, district director of instructional services, and approved by Superintendent of Schools, Dr. George Roberts.

Thus the controversy was put to rest, at least for the summer.

PART TWO
Roles and Actions

CHAPTER FOUR

THE PARENT

This chapter and the three that follow are examinations of the roles and actions of the key players in the book controversy. The chapters follow the order in which four individuals emerged during the unfolding of the controversy. First is the parent, who initiated the controversy by making the protest at the Community Input Session. Chapter 5 is focused on the role of the superintendent, whose actions in response to the protest moved the controversy forward. The role of the substitute teacher, who found herself defending her assignment of the controversial book, is considered in Chapter 6. Finally, in Chapter 7, I examine the role and actions of the director, who took charge of processing the complaint and resolving the controversy.

The parent's role in the *Go Ask Alice* controversy was more complicated than it may appear from the chronology of events. Two important facts must be considered. First, earlier in the school year, the parent, John Andrews, had protested the assignment of the novel, *The Disappearance*. He had handled that protest differently. He had simply called the teacher and requested that his daughter be allowed to read a different book. The request had been granted. Therefore, before the assignment of *Go Ask Alice* was made, he knew who to contact and what to say if he objected to an assigned book.

However, when he reflected on his complaint concerning the first book, Andrews felt that the principal did not follow up on the larger question about the use of *The Disappearance* in his child's school. When interviewed for this study, Andrews commented,

> I think I was a little bit disappointed in the principal there at Lincoln Middle School, because the first time I requested that a change be made, I never heard from the principal [pause] at all. The classroom teacher responded and gave her [the daughter] an alternate reading source.

A second fact does not appear in the chronology. That is, Andrews was already planning to attend the Community Input Session of May 5 *before* he became aware that his daughter was reading *Go Ask Alice*. He said:

> I received a call from a gal in the community who wanted to go to the school board with some questionable material and there happened to be one of those community input sessions scheduled for that next week, and [she] wanted to know if I would go and kind of support her in what she was doing, and things like that, as a group of concerned parents. And I said, well, I'd be happy to go along.

Andrews didn't remember which books or materials were considered questionable by the group that he was asked to support. However, presenting his protest to the board of education was not a spontaneous act. He knew that others had planned to make similar protests, and he had personally processed a protest of a book earlier in the school year.

During the interviews, it also became clear that Andrews recognized that his actions in the controversy involved more than one role. For example, when Andrews spoke at the Community Input Session, he believed that he was acting as a parent and as a citizen and taxpayer, even though most of the people at the meeting knew him as a teacher of speech and English at one of the district's two high schools. As his interpretation of events unfolded, Andrews came to view the controversy from two distinct perspectives: parent *and* teacher. And as the controversy grew, he found that those two perspectives overlapped and caused some problems for him.

In fact, during the interviews, one of the themes that Andrews developed was his recognition that the two roles were not easily separated at all. While he maintained that his actions *as a parent* were correct, he questioned his actions in terms of his role as a teacher — or, more accurately, as a member of the district's professional staff. Therefore, it will be useful to examine both of these roles.

The Parent Role

Andrews became aware that his daughter was reading *Go Ask Alice* as they were driving to the airport because his daughter read some paragraphs from the novel to him while they were traveling. After hearing the excerpts, Andrews decided to protest the book's use in his daughter's classroom. His motives in acting to prevent the use of *Go Ask Alice* were summarized when he said:

> [B]ecause of the real [verbal emphasis] vile language in that one section of that book, I didn't feel it was appropriate for anybody. I thought somebody should say something. And most of those kids are reading that book and they're either calloused to it, they don't care, and most parents aren't aware of what their kids are reading anyway. I just happened to have a daughter that came home and shared with me what she was reading.

As Andrews had intended to attend the board of education meeting of May 5 before he learned that his daughter was reading *Go Ask Alice,* he chose to voice his own protest at the Community Input Session because he sensed, in his words, "There's the vehicle I could use to bring this to the attention of the board."

After reading the excerpt at the meeting, he knew that his protest had a profound effect on the members of the board of education and the spectators in the audience. He described the reading with these words:

> When I read that passage, you could have heard a pin drop in that room. I mean, it was just — 'cause I don't think

anybody realized that that book contained, you know, that kind of language . . . And Dr. Roberts looked at me and he said, "That book will be gone tomorrow." I sat down and that was the end of it.

After he read the excerpts, the others in the group that had planned to make a protest did not do so. When asked about the woman who had asked him to attend, Andrews said, "She didn't even speak. After I was done, she said, 'you did so much more than I could've done' [laughs]."

Andrews recognized that he had created a moment of drama, but he was surprised by the superintendent's action. Before making his protest, he had felt that the input sessions were more for information gathering than for developing a course of action. He said:

I didn't expect it to be a big explosion — I expected a community input session. I expected their reaction to say, well, we'll take care of that book, thank you very much. That would've been the end of it, but . . . So that's [laughs], that's what happened.

After the input session ended, reporters from the newspaper and radio stations interviewed Andrews. As the media began focusing on the protest, Andrews became aware that his actions were going to have greater effects than he anticipated. He described the actions of the media:

After the meeting, I was jumped on by at least one reporter from the *Newport Press* and two local radio stations wanting to know the title of the book, the author of the book, why I felt the way I did, da-da, da-da, da-da — the whole thing. Then I realized how out of proportion this thing was going to get the next morning when I came to school and people here said, "Hey, I heard you on the radio this morning," because some of the reporters had quoted me with their cassette recorders, and that was on the radio that morning. That evening in the *Newport Press*, it was "High School Teacher Has Textbook Banned." Banner headline across the

Press — the whole rest of the Community Input Session was back on page 8 somewhere — but that made the headlines of the *Press*, which I was a little bit disgusted that they would pick that. . . . And I guess I realized that censorship is such a volatile issue that, you know, that hit — and I did not intend that when I went. I went as a concerned parent. I didn't even go as a teacher. I went as a concerned parent.

Andrews reported receiving feedback from other parents and citizens. As he discussed the various forms of feedback, he said:

I was also concerned about the rest of the class and/or classes in the future, that were, you know, being asked to read this book. Well then, the response of many people in the community is, what business is that of yours? Who made you the watchguard for society? . . . We got a number of comments — at the time I was coaching fifth- and sixth-grade boys — a number of parents, of course, knew what I had done and came up to me and said, "Way to go, it's about time somebody takes a stand. I'm glad somebody's watching out for things like that."

He also received requests from people he didn't know, who wanted him to represent their causes. Andrews said:

I got a few phone calls from people I didn't even know. [pause] Interesting, I got one call — two calls — from people that wanted me to go to the school board on their behalf, speaking about a cause that they have. And I said, you really feel strongly about this? "Yes." I said, I got a recommendation for you. "Oh, what's that?" I said, you go to the school board and you tell 'em. I said I'm not going to stand on anybody's pedestal for them. I said, this [*Go Ask Alice* protest] was something personal for me that I felt strongly about. "Well, we're just looking for a spokesperson." [laughs] I said, No — I'm sorry. I said, I'm sorry. I'm not into that. I said, if you've got a good issue that you feel strongly about, then you go to the school board and you talk to them about that.

As the controversy continued to grow, Andrews became worried about the effect that it might have on his daughter. He reported that his daughter had received feedback about his appearance before the board of education and the news reports that followed. He said:

> She got mixed reactions from her friends that are. . . some badgering and some, you know, kidding and things like that. And there were also a number of friends that came up to her and said, "Good, I hated reading that. And I'm glad somebody said something." Yet they [other students] never go home and tell their own parents. So it was kind of mixed. And she took it real well. You know, after this whole thing blew up in the paper, I thought, Oh no. Here's my daughter, a seventh-grader, and now she's gotta put up with all that abuse from her friends and that. But she really took it well. She came home and said, "I'm getting some kidding but its not. . . . [gesture: shrugged shoulders, palms of hands up indicates insignificance]

The complexity of the parent's role is highlighted in the events of June 15, when the Supplementary Materials Review Committee met. As reported in the chronology, Andrews was notified by letter of the meeting's purpose, location, and date. Both Andrews and his wife addressed the committee. During our second interview, he admitted that both he and his wife were very concerned about the meeting. He said:

> We were very cautious about it. In the review session, [we] would not become argumentative. And Mary [wife] and I really prayed about it before we went in, and we're not gonna become argumentative. . . . We didn't know what we were up against in there. We didn't know if we were gonna go in there and five people put us against the wall with submachine guns or what, you know. We just wanted to go in and just calmly present our case, and we did not want to become argumentative.

Andrews summarized the Supplementary Materials Review Committee:

Dr. Olson's [the director] role was to moderate the review committee, and they met with my wife and I in — would've been in June. And we reviewed the entire procedure, and the end result of that review was — there were mixed emotions. Some people on the review committee thought the book should be taught — nothing wrong with what was in that book.

Andrews said that some committee members made two main arguments for retaining the use of the book: its usefulness in drug education and as an example of the diary technique in literature. Commented Andrews:

Some people thought that the book should be offered because they were trying to teach the diary technique, which is why that book is being offered. Our contention was, perhaps there's another book out there that has better content that they could use to teach the diary technique rather than that one, because of the language that was in it.

Andrews also was concerned about how the book's descriptions of sexual activities would be handled as part of the classroom discussions. He posed this question to those who advocated the use of *Go Ask Alice*:

How do you explain, for example, when she says, you know, "Then Frank and I went on and had a blow job"? How do you explain that to your class when they ask you, what is that? "Well, we kind of just, uh, uh, . . ." I say, come on, you're dealing with eighth-graders, or seventh-graders. What do you tell them? You know, I mean, it's right there. "Well, we don't focus on that." I said, you may not, but what do the kids think when they are reading that? So on and so forth.

Andrews said that he and his wife felt that their experiences in the meeting were positive. As a result of that meeting, both parents understood that *Go Ask Alice* would not be used in the classroom. Andrews said:

Anyway, the bottom line was that the book should not be taught in the middle school level. That's what they said. It would not be pulled from the library because if students wanted to read it on an individual basis, fine. But it would not be used as a classroom assignment. It should be removed from the reading list.

Being a teacher, Andrews also was aware that school district personnel needed to update the reading lists. He said:

The offshoot of this was also that a committee was going to be formed to review that reading list because nobody had any record — and Tom Baker [districtwide chair of the Language Arts Department] searched and searched and searched as to when that book was ever approved to be on that reading list. And one of the things that we discovered through this whole process was that there were many books that were on the approved reading list for classroom use in the middle school that nowhere on record was there ever any written approval, or who approved it, or whoever reviewed it, or anything. They just somehow got on that list. And because we went back to see where *Go Ask Alice* was first approved and by whom, and nobody had any record of it. So after that it was suggested by Dr. Olson that they go back and review that recommended reading list for the middle school, and see if perhaps there's some newer material that could be added, to replace some things that were on there. And after that I've heard nothing since.

Ironically, of the key players, the parent is the only one who recognized how the controversy was affecting the classroom teacher who had assigned the reading. Neither the superintendent nor the director mentioned anything about the classroom teacher. The parent said:

Oh, the teacher involved was also there. Unfortunately she was a long-term sub, and she was just beside herself thinking, I'm never gonna get a job in the Newport school system again as a result of this . . . .

After the decision of the Supplementary Materials Review Committee became public, Andrews was contacted by the press for a comment. Because he viewed his experience with the media on May 5 as being negative, he chose not to comment. Andrews reported:

> We got a call from the *Newport Press* asking about the decision of the committee and if we had any comment. And I had no comment for them. I directed them to Dr. Olson. I did not feel as though I wanted to talk to the Press any more except that I said I was satisfied with the decision that was made.

The Teacher Role

Before he attended the Community Input Session, Andrews was aware that his two roles, parent and teacher, could become problematic. Although he did not define those potential problems, he sensed that his actions might put him in conflict with some latent institutional rules that seem to be at work in the school district. In fact, he recalled discussing this issue with his wife:

> Maybe as a teacher, maybe I shouldn't be doing this. Maybe you should. . . I remember saying those words. And she looked at me and before she could respond — and I know what she would have said. She would have said, "Well, if you feel that way, I'll do it." But before she ever said that, I said, "Before I'm a teacher, I'm a parent. And as a parent, I have a right and an obligation to do this. And I will do it, and I need to take that stand. I can't back down. I believe it's my obligation."

Some of the latent rules in effect in the Newport School District were revealed as the parent described his role in the controversy from the perspective of being a member of the professional staff. Although these latent rules were not specified, the "known but unwritten" understandings regarding how the school system was to operate were important factors in the Andrews' actions. For example, he recognized that his public protest might have some general negative effect on the entire school district. He commented:

> What does it look like when somebody within the system rips apart the system.? That just does not look good, and if anything we need positive PR. We don't need negativism coming from within the ranks. And here this guy goes and puts his foot in his mouth — and headlines — teacher does this, you know.

After he had protested the use of *Go Ask Alice*, Andrews also realized that many of his fellow workers were upset with him. He felt that the greatest source of their concern came from the way in which he protested the book, not from the substance of his protest. He commented:

> I think people were more upset, not with the fact that I protested a book, but that I didn't go through what they thought as an educator — you should know the proper channels to go through and why did you make such a big explosive thing out of it?

Andrews reported that on two occasions he had an opportunity to explain his actions to the superintendent. The first came when the superintendent contacted him. The parent reported that the main point made by the superintendent on that occasion was that the protest should have been made through the procedures available within the system. He quoted the superintendent as saying, "I only wish you had come to me personally. . . . We could have dealt with this one-on-one, and that would've taken care of it."

The second opportunity to talk with the superintendent occurred when the parent asked to have a conference with him because he felt that it was necessary to separate his two roles from one another. When he met with the superintendent and the director, Andrews described the purpose of that meeting:

> Just to be sure that we had an understanding about why I did what I did, and why I chose to take that route, we met

one afternoon. It was about an hour, and they understood why I as a parent decided to take that route, and they still expressed the desire that, as a person working in the system, it probably would've been better had I gone directly to Dr. Roberts [the superintendent] rather than using the vehicle of the Community Input Session. However, they said, as a parent, you certainly have a right to use that vehicle. That's open to you as it is open to anybody else.

Besides wanting another chance to explain his actions and wanting to find out what recriminations might occur as a result of making his protest public, Andrews also realized that he might have jeopardized some of his own programs by making a public protest. In a discussion with his building principal, he attempted to get that administrator's opinion about how the board of education would respond if he had to ask for funding for a special program. He reported that conversation by saying:

> [I asked,] Do you think this is going to have any impact down the road? Like, if I go to the school board for funding a project. . . are they going to remember this? And he said, "It's quite possible that they might." And, I said, "Well, what they do, they do." I said, "I've not felt any repercussions like that."

At the time of the interviews for this study, about two years after the controversy, there had been no repercussions from the board of education. However, Andrews had encountered some hostility from his fellow workers. During the interview, he described two types of hostility: direct and subtle. Direct hostility came from fellow teachers in the form of confrontations; however, the subtle repercussions were the most difficult to handle because they were done in silence. He reported, for example, that on the day after the Community Input Session, three people stopped in his office and commented on his protest:

> I got reactions — everything from "I understand" — everything from no response at all. I mean, there were a number of people that never said a word to me about it. Two,

[pause] I had two people come to my [office] door the next morning. One of them stuck their head in my door and said, "I just want to let you know you just set education back ten years. I thought we were friends. I don't know how you could do this to us," and turned around and walked out. That person and I are now very much on good speaking terms and no problem whatsoever.

I had another person come to me who obviously is very vehement about censorship and said, "You just gave me the worst day of my entire life as an educator," and turned around and walked out. And I thought that my response to those people had to be that life goes on as usual. And I can not see these people coming up the steps — I can't turn and walk away because I know they have something against me. And in both cases I continue to treat those people as I always had — continue to greet them with a good morning and everything else. And in both cases the friendship we had beforehand has been totally restored and there's no animosity or anything left anymore. I heard rumors about this faculty lounge was really chastising me — at this school or at that school. [Pause] There were times after that that I walked into our faculty lounge and all of a sudden I'd hear conversation stop and all of a sudden I thought, I wonder if they were talking about me before I walked in here.

It took months for me to get over that. I'd walk down a hall and I'd see two teachers, two or three teachers standing in a little group talking like you do any other time. And as I would walk past, my ear would kinda go like — [pause]. I wonder if they were talking about me. I was really self-conscious of that, you know. And there were even a few people in the language arts department that said, "I don't necessarily agree with what you did, but I support your right to be able to do that."

Some of the faculty members felt that the parent had acted from his religious principles rather than any parenting principles. One faculty member that I interviewed believed that Andrews' actions in protesting *Go Ask Alice* represented a broader agenda. This individual commented:

> It was a group of people who were behind this [the controversy] — fundamentalists. And it was more than a book. They had been looking at many different things. And, uh, it was one of these deals where the next thing was — we want the teachers' lesson plans. . . .

The parent understood that some faculty members were afraid that he might be representing a group from outside the school district, and that faculty members thought that the outside group intended to purge the schools of reading materials like *Go Ask Alice*. During our interview Andrews said:

> Another teacher came to my door and just said, "I just need to know for my own benefit, did you do this as an individual, or are you part of a group that's starting a movement?" And I looked at him and said, it's strictly one father's concern for a reading assignment that his daughter had. It's no part of any group or movement. He said, "Thank you, I needed to know that." And he turned and he walked out. . . . And I thought about that after a while, and then I realized probably where he was coming from. Because a lot of people know of my Christian faith, and thought that maybe I was starting a big censorship movement or was part of a group that was gonna start cleaning out the school system, looking for dirty laundry all over the place, and start — like a group moves through and cleans all the *Playboys* out of the mini-marts in town. Another group comes through and gets rid of all the R-rated videos. Here's Andrews with his group coming through and cleaning out all the — [pause]. And it wasn't that at all. And then I realized, I bet those rumors were spreading. I never heard them. But I can imagine people were having a great time talking about, yeah, Andrews is president of some group that's coming in. You could — [pause] you know how rumors go.

The parent's classroom and office are across the hall from the library. Glass-fronted cases display available books and students' projects that have been completed in the library. The parent reported that during the week designated as "Drug Education Week," the librarian included *Go Ask Alice* as one of the books in her thematic display. As a result of this display, the parent received some feedback from his students. He reported:

> We had a drug education week or whatever, that book was on display [laughs]. In our display case right over here, as one that students should read. Right across from my classrooms. I heard kids say, "Right under your nose, right?" I thought, that's — that's okay. I'm not, you know, — [laughs] I just refused to get into personal conflicts with that.

The parent also realized that the positive responses he received for his protest were for his role as a parent. Those individuals, according to Andrews, said, "It's nice to see a parent take a stand."

Indeed, the parent's Christian faith is broadly recognized by his colleagues because Andrews unhesitatingly includes references to it in his conversations. During the interview, for example, he explained how his faith helped in preparing for the Supplementary Materials Review Committee. He said, "Mary [his wife] and I really prayed about it before we went in, and said we're not going to become argumentative."

The parent also was aware that some of the people at the Supplementary Materials Review Committee meeting were antagonistic toward him and his protest. For example, he described one person's reaction by saying:

> One middle school librarian, she was really adamant about any kind of censorship. It was just [pause] you could just see walking in that she was [growls]. Right in the introductions, I mean she just [laughs]. I could just sense that there's — that gal was really — was really bitter. And I felt sorry for her to be that bitter, you know, that closed-minded.

Retrospective

In reviewing his role in the controversy at a distance of two years, the parent still felt strongly that the book should not be used in the classroom. However, in the event of another protest, he said that he would use different tactics. Also, although he did not directly identify them, he appeared to have been reminded of the latent rules that govern protests within the institutional system.

Following is Andrews' capsule re-evaluation of the controversy, the use of *Go Ask Alice* , and the processes he used in making the protest:

> See, I don't think that book should be taught as a classroom set. If individuals want to read it, it's there — they can read it. Because, see, if you check out a book and you read it — they can read it. If a student reads that book as a book report for your class and they get to that part and they find that offensive and they don't want to read it, they take the book back to the library and they're done with it. . . . But when it's assigned by a teacher, many kids aren't gonna question that. They're just gonna sit and they're gonna read the whole thing, and that's it. Now are kids not exposed to that kind of language? Come on, I'm not that naive. Kids have heard that before. Okay? And half the kids have probably been through some of the stuff she talked about. But that's not the point. . . . And the one thing I said, would you, if kids talked like this in the hallways at Lincoln, what would happen then? The principal looked at me and said, "They'd be suspended." They'd be suspended for using that language but yet you'll let 'em read it in their English class. I said, somewhere we've got a contradiction here. He said, "Yeah, you're right."

Andrews confirmed his surprise at the superintendent's immediate reaction to his protest. But as he explained his own reaction to the superintendent's removal of the book, Andrews still hadn't recognized the importance of the superintendent's action. Andrews said:

> I thought he reacted a little bit hastily. I don't think he should have jumped up at that meeting and said that book will be gone. That just — whoa! . . . I definitely lit the fuse, but that just, you know, made it go off. And I really wish he

would've just stood up and said, "We will review this matter very rapidly," or whatever, and then sat down, and then asked to see me afterwards. You know, made a few phone calls to the schools the next day when the press wasn't there and said, perhaps we ought to take a look at that book, pull it off the shelves until we can review it. And then we'll decide what we're gonna do about it, you know. . . . But just this instant banning of the book was like, you know, [pause]. Of course, what I read was rather shocking, too, so . . . [laughs] . . . I don't know what kind of power the superintendent has. You know, I suppose he can do that. But I — I just thought it was a little bit reactionary.

And, even though Andrews hadn't changed his mind about the use of the novel, he had changed his mind about the process he used to make his protest. As a result of his earlier protest of *The Disappearance*, his daughter had been given an alternative reading assignment. At the time of the interview, two years after the *Go Ask Alice* controversy, Andrews said that if he needed to protest another book, he would process the protest differently, reverting for the most part to the more direct approach he had used in the earlier protest:

If she were to come in with something from your English class, for example, something that we didn't think was appropriate, I'd go directly to you. Because I've always known and everything I've ever been taught — and I believe this is also biblical — you're to go right to that person and deal with that issue. And especially being in this building. Even if she were at Washington High, I'd pick up the phone right away and I'd ask to talk to that teacher and say, Hey, my daughter's been given this assignment. I don't want to make a big deal out of it. I'm gonna request an alternate assignment. And if the teacher would refuse, then I'd go to the building principal. If the building principal would refuse, then I'd go right to Dr. Roberts. . . . I would — I would go directly to the teacher, as I did the first time. It just so happened that the timing on this — when she read that to me in the car — the very next night, I'd already planned on going to the community input session and talking about that very issue. Now I had a piece of evidence in my hand. So it's just — the timing was right there.

Finally, the best summary of Andrews's reaction to the *Go Ask Alice* controversy is with his own words:

I don't look at it as the black mark in my educational career. I'm not proud of the publicity that it got, and I wish it wouldn't have gotten that. And I'm not happy with the fact that some of my peers felt negative about it, because I'm the kind of guy, although I won't go out of my way to create this, I do enjoy being liked by people. You know, and I think basically teachers enjoy being liked by their class, so on and so forth, you know. And I don't like doing something that's gonna create animosity amongst my peers. But yet as a parent — I've said this a thousand times — I knew I had the right and I had to take a stand. And I had to do something about that.

CHAPTER FIVE

THE SUPERINTENDENT

George Roberts became superintendent of the Newport Area School District in 1982. His professional experience included classroom teaching, athletic coaching, curriculum development, and district administration. He was completing his fifth year in the school district when the *Go Ask Alice* controversy occurred.

For this project, I interviewed Roberts twice. About one year elapsed between the first interview and the second. When the first interview began, he pulled a chair around to the front of his desk, handed me his file on the controversy, and talked casually about the incident. Like the parent, the superintendent seemed eager for his actions during the *Go Ask Alice* controversy to be understood. At the second interview, Roberts displayed a far different attitude. He was late for the second interview. As the interview began, his first words were, "How long is this going to take?" In the middle of one of the questions, he wrote a note to himself about some other topic. The note was placed on his desk and not referred to during the interview. Controversy about books and researchers who are interested in such controversy apparently had become an insignificant issue to an administrator who must allot his time to the general maintenance of a school district with a $44 million budget.

In the following excerpt from the first interview, Roberts recounts the activities of 5 May 1987, providing his own interpretation of his actions and a sense of his own administrative philosophy. He said:

Let me go through how I did it, how I can recall it to the best of my knowledge; how I would second guess myself. First of all in view of the policy that [when] there is no policy the superintendent makes the decision — so that night was a community input session, and I don't remember how many people were there. Could have been 50; could have been 100. And John Andrews got up and he said, I object to the requirement that my daughter has to read a book in Lincoln Middle School called *Go Ask Alice*, and I would like to read several passages from the book to this audience. And he read the passages and, if I remember right, there was "cocksucker," there was "fucker" and other types of words, and sitting there I could just see the board members cringe [laughs]. I could also see people in the audience cringe.

Roberts suggested that the genesis of his decision to remove the book began with his reaction to Andrews' reading. He recalled:

Personally, I guess I had to say, what are my values as the superintendent? And I said, that book will not be read. I made that statement. It will be off the shelf tomorrow, and we'll take a look at it.

Two years after the incident, the superintendent recognized that he should have considered alternatives to removing the book. As he recalled the incident, a sense of the personal frustration that the incident had caused became noticeable. The superintendent spoke rhetorically when he said:

What I should have done — I should have said, we have a procedure for filing a complaint of the textbook policy; why don't you do that? Why did you choose to sensationalize your objection rather than go through the procedure? That's what I should have done, but I didn't. Okay, did I shoot a hole in my foot? Maybe. On the same side of the coin I was able to give a message: If you have values — moral and ethical values regarding the type of conduct, the type of school district we want to have, this was the opportunity for me to give it, recognizing after I said all those things that I'm going to get shot at. [pause] It's one of those you can't win. I said to myself, well, you'll probably have the ACLU, you will have the English teachers saying you have taken away my rights, my liberties, you'll have all these other types of things. On the other side of the coin, I knew that I would get support from people who want us to have a good school system.

Roberts reported that it had been part of his plan to review the policies of the board of education during the morning of May 6:

The next morning I got together with Martin [the director] and I said, I know we have a policy on this; please review with me what the policy says. So we reviewed the policy, and the procedure should have been like I said. I should have said, If you have a complaint, here's the procedure. So obviously I was contacted by a lot of people the next day, and what I did was I temporarily suspended the use of that book. I wrote a memo to the board that I was temporarily pulling that book, pending further investigation. If I find that the book is appropriate, it will go back on the shelf. If I find it inappropriate. . . . [pause] As we look to the use of that textbook, I believe that it was not required. I believe it was a supplementary book, and another book could have been used by the student if they had an objection. That morning I also contacted all three middle schools and said that book was temporarily suspended from use and to hold off until investigation is completed.

The superintendent's reaction to the May 5 reading of excerpts from *Go Ask Alice* was prompted by his perceptions of reactions from the board and members of the audience. He reacted in part to the reactions of others. He sensed that they expected him to take a specific action rather than refer the matter for action at a later date by an anonymous committee. He apparently felt responsible for having allowed this book to be read and decided, therefore, that only immediate action, removing the book, would restore his credibility as head of the institution. His comment, "First of all, in view of the policy that when there is no policy, the superintendent makes the decision . . ." reflects both his sense of responsibility as the leader of the district and his sense of power as holder of the highest administrative position.

His "when there is no policy" comment also suggests that he did not know that there was a policy for handling book protests. Not being aware of a specific policy within the district might at first glance appear to be a weakness, in that administrators are supposed to be guided by the policies of the district. However, the Newport Area School District has more than 550 policies, supplemented by an equal number of administrative rules and regulations, which in turn are supplemented by various types of exhibits. All of the district's administrators have complete copies of both the policies and the rules and regulations. The policies are organized by the McKell-Davies coding system. In this system, policies dealing with instruction are in the 600 series; those policies are enacted by the director of instructional services, who reports to the superintendent.

Nonetheless, after the superintendent had been briefed on the policies and knew that his action was contrary to policy, he followed through on his decision. He called the middle school principals and directed that the books be removed from the classrooms and the libraries.

Roberts knew that he had extended his power beyond the board policies. Two years after the controversy, he found two justifications for his actions. First, he had the impression that the Supplementary Materials Review Committee had decided that he had been correct. Second, he felt that if he had not taken direct action, one or several of the school board members might have acted without administrative input. About the Supplementary Materials Review Committee, he said:

> I asked Martin to reconvene the review committee according to the policy. They reviewed the book; they came back with the decision that that book should not be used as a supplementary text. So consequently, they supported what I had done. I hope that they did that being pure and clean in

their rationale and decision-making process; I wouldn't want them to rubber stamp me and say, Well, we took him out of the hot-bed box, you know. If they had not supported it, I would have had a tough time myself, because I would have had to support the policy and I would have had to explain that to the board. The board probably would have jumped in and changed the policy, and we could have the *Go Ask Alice* situation all over. And I try to keep those things in a rational decision-making process rather than [pause]. So I think that's how the procedure unfolded.

The superintendent's second justification for acting beyond board policy was that by doing so he took the initiative to act away from members of the board of education. In short, he was acting to maintain control rather than risking a loss of control to the board and being directed by them. He explained:

That's another reason why I made the decision so quick, that took the board out of it. They wouldn't get involved. I don't recall exactly who was on the board at that time, but I do know that there were some people who would have done that. They would have done it. Some may have done it for political or ego purposes to make themselves look good. I didn't do it to make myself look good, because I knew I was going to get shot from both sides; I've been in those situations before.

A third line of reasoning also emerged during the interview. As mentioned earlier, the response of the audience provided an important cue to Roberts that he should act. During his administration, he had made himself accessible to the community in various ways, meeting with citizens' groups regularly. It was his contention that if it were necessary, he would have means to explain his actions to other members of the community so that repercussions would be minimal. He said:

I also knew that I could review these materials with other groups that I do meet. For example, I meet with the clergy on a regular basis. And we talked about censorship with them. You'd be surprised; they're very supportive of not having a lot of censorship; and, they do believe in a democratic society, and yet they also recognize the political arena in which they operate. So, yes, the board could have jumped in and done something drastic.

Even though the parent was also a teacher, the superintendent thought that the controversy would have had to be handled in the fashion it was. About the parent's protest at the Community Input Session, the superintendent said:

> He [the parent] came as a citizen and as a parent. He should have known the rules better than a parent, but it was my responsibility that night to say, you do have a policy; this is what you should go through and file your complaint. And as I sat down with Martin [the director of instruction] after that session, a couple of days later we talked about had we had any people file complaints about books and materials we're using; we have had some that had. It's a question of type of objection. In fact, John [the parent] had filed an objection to some other materials that had been in use, and his daughter had been given something else to read, as the policy provides. But you have to treat an employee just like any other citizen with children in our system, otherwise it wouldn't be fair to them.

Note in this comment Robert's use of the term "rules." The rules to which he refers are latent, or unstated but understood. Such "rules" contrast with manifest rules, which may be stated in policies or guidelines. Chapter 8 is devoted to a discussion of latent and manifest rules and results, because they are a key dimension in the analysis of the *Go Ask Alice* controversy.

Although the *Go Ask Alice* controversy amounted to a major school governance issue, many of the administrators, including the superintendent, labeled it a "side issue." Roberts explained, "It's like you're trying to run the mile, and you've got this side ache; it's something that's going to take away from your efficiency to do other things." As an administrator, he expected side issues to occur. He said:

You try to forecast what are the side issues. For example, at our administrative staff meetings that we've had so far this year, we say, have you picked up any side issues that you anticipate may be coming up? And we list those things and we try to get those things resolved before they mushroom into something bigger.

Viewing the *Go Ask Alice* controversy as a side issue is an important perspective because it differs from the perspective of the teachers who were involved in the controversy. The side-issue perspective led the administrators to act in a manner that seemed to exacerbate the controversy from the teachers' view.

I mentioned at the start of this chapter that the superintendent's degree of interest in this research project differed from first interview to the second. In the year between the two interviews, the voters of the community had rejected two building referenda that were initiated by the administration and the board of education. Speakers at other Community Input Sessions, as well as writers of letters to the *Newport Press,* had been critical of the superintendent's actions in the management of the school district. In part it can be said that other issues, such as building utilization, staffing ratios, construction costs, program cuts, and land disposition and acquisition, had accumulated. These problems proved far more demanding of administrative time than reminiscing about the *Go Ask Alice* controversy.

CHAPTER SIX

THE TEACHER

Teacher Rachel Hansen assigned the reading of *Go Ask Alice*. She was a long-term substitute teacher for the regular classroom teacher, who was on disability leave. As a long-term substitute teacher, her role in the controversy was different from the role that would have been played by a regular member of the professional staff.

After her two children reached school age, Hansen had returned to college and earned a degree from the University of Wisconsin-Milwaukee in 1986. Before she returned to college, her educational experiences in Newport included graduating from Washington High School, working as a mother's helper at an elementary school, and helping the parent-teacher organization at her sons' schools. To supplement the family income, she worked as a secretary at her church.

As a long-term resident of Newport, and as a long-term participant in the educational processes of the school district, Hansen was aware of local mores and norms. As a substitute teacher who became embroiled in a well-publicized controversy, she also understood that her potential career as a full-time teacher might be in jeopardy. The importance of the controversy to Hansen can be summarized with her remark, "I thought for sure my career was over before it began."

By definition, a substitute teacher is lower in status in the school's internal society than regular classroom teachers, part-time teachers, and teachers' aides. Substitute teachers do not belong to the teachers union; individuals in the other three groups do. The turnover of substitutes makes it difficult for them to maintain an effective alternative organization, even though a formal association does exist for substitute teachers. Consequently, being a substitute teacher put Hansen in a more difficult position than a regular teacher might have faced in similar circumstances.

The days between May 5 and June 15 were traumatic for Hansen. She reported:

> I felt very alone; like I had nothing. I had no union; I had nothing to back me, not a thing. I didn't know what I — you know — what was going to happen. And, I thought, this man [the parent] who is a professional is taking me for a ride; and he did.

Four themes stand out regarding Hansen's role in the *Go Ask Alice* controversy. First, according to the documents and the interviews given by the other players in the controversy, Hansen was not considered a significant player. Second, she became a substitute to get a full-time job with regular employment and benefits. Third, she felt that the parent had treated her unfairly. She had satisfied his earlier request regarding the assignment of *The Disappearance,* and she thought she should have had the same chance with the assignment of *Go Ask Alice.* She also felt that as a professional peer, the parent should have been more thoughtful about the effects his protest would have on a fellow teacher. Fourth, the manner in which the controversy was handled indicated to her that she had been wrong in her actions as a person and as a professional. Each of these themes merits further exploration.

Hansen was not treated as a significant player in the *Go Ask Alice* controversy, except possibly by her principal, who sought her help in developing his report. According to her perspective on the controversy, she also was not considered a significant participant in the controversy's resolution. With the exception of the letter that she submitted, none of the documents in the superintendent's file mention her name, nor are any of the memos addressed to her. In fact, her invitation to attend the Supplementary Materials Review Committee meeting was issued in a offhand statement to her principal. The memo addressed to the principal read, "You and/or your teacher, of course, may attend the review, if you wish."

Even the way that Hansen found out about the controversy was offhand. For instance, no one telephoned her after the Community Input Session. In fact, she became aware of the *Go Ask Alice* controversy only as she listened to the radio news while driving to work at Lincoln Middle School the next morning, May 6. When she arrived at the school, she found many of her co-workers upset by the news reports. She also received various instructions as she entered the building. Hansen said:

> The following day as I was driving to work, I heard the news that Mr. John Andrews had gone to the board of education and told them all about these things. And the next thing I knew, I got to school and people came running into my room saying, if any newspaper people or if any — helicopter, whatever, lands out in the field and they want to talk to you, tell them you have no comment. I'm going, Okay. Petrified. Totally petrified.

Hansen did not remember whether the principal or assistant principal came to her classroom and collected the copies of *Go Ask Alice*. She simply said that her instructions were:

> Just say, "no comment" and collect the books immediately . . . because the directive had come from the board of education that they had to be turned in. Now I had some students who didn't have the book there, and they were sent home to get them. . . . They had to have those books either brought in by a parent, or they had to go home and get them.

In our interview, Hansen said that she had a mixed reaction to the superintendent's order that the books be collected:

> I think he was probably reacting to, you know, what happened. I don't know. I don't think that's policy. That you set

up policies to follow policy, and I don't think that's a policy that he can just pull it off the shelf like that. I don't know. How was my reaction to that? I guess I was really numb. I really didn't think one way or the other. I really didn't think anything; it was just so fast. So quick. And it was over and done with, you know, I mean, it was just too much at one time. I was so worried about other things that that was the last thing on my mind — that they were pulling it off the shelves. I wasn't happy about it.

From Hansen's point of view, the intensity of the reaction to the controversy by the school personnel was the result of two problems: 1) the personnel were unprepared for the controversy and 2) the controversy was initiated by a member the district's own staff. She said:

Probably because they didn't really know what was going on. They were caught off guard. . . . This man is to be a professional, and I guess he caught them off guard, and he had complained — I had passed out a book previous to that [passing out *Go Ask Alice*] when I was working and he had not liked that [*The Disappearance*]. . . . And he called and said that he didn't think that that was appropriate; and I said, fine. While we're discussing it, I'll have her out of the room; she can be in the library, and she can read a different book of her choice.

During the interview sessions, the teacher continually referred to the fact that the parent did not contact her and register his complaint. He had used that method before, and his wishes had been granted. She also felt that, in his role as a teacher, he should have had the professional courtesy to contact her before he addressed the board of education. Hansen commented:

I had assumed that if he did not feel this [*Go Ask Alice*] was appropriate, he could've at least called me. But he chose to do it along other lines. . . . I think he should've called me again, and should've said, I don't think its appropriate. Then he could have gone through the whole process when you disagree with a book, or you think a book should be pulled from the shelves, or whatever. There's a certain process that all teachers, or all people have to follow. And he chose not to do that, follow that procedure. Why, I don't know.

Later in the interview, she again referred to her chagrin at the way the parent had processed his protest. This time, she felt that he had a professional responsibility to uphold. She believed that his failure to treat her as a professional implied that she was guilty of some wrongdoing. She said:

> Even for him, to not check it out first — I mean, he must have lesson plans and thoughts into what he is doing, and to think that I just would — you know. That's the assumption I was under. That if he disapproved of it, that's one thing. And I have many, you know, who disapprove of who knows what. And that's fine; they can do that, I don't mind. But you let me know about it. You can tell me about it, and then we'll see what we can do to change it; you just don't take it, you know, right away to the top and say, this is what this person is doing. Yeah, it was implied guilt, most definitely.

When the director sent a memo to the principal of Lincoln Middle School, it was addressed only to the principal; however, the responsibility to provide the requested information was given to the reading consultant and to Hansen. She described the scene:

> John [the reading consultant] comes up to me and he says, you know we have to do this [provide information about assigning Go Ask Alice]. That was from Martin [the director], and we had to write all kinds of things. And I'm going, "Oh, my God." So I came home and I told my husband all of this stuff and he says, you know, the best thing for you to do is to talk to someone. And he has his own business, so he has his own attorney. So he says, why don't you just go talk to him? So I said, well, I've got nothing to lose. . . . So I went and talked to him. And then he saw this [the memo requesting information], and he said, this is fine and dandy; you can fill this out with Mr. Winston [the reading consultant], but

69

you write your own paper: what you were gonna do, what led up to it, and everything else in detail, you know, with any information that you can find. Which is what I did.

The product of the lawyer's recommendation was the letter that Hansen sent to the director, dated June 10. The memo sent to the director from the principal informing the director about the use of the novel was sent on June 9. The teacher's name was not included as having contributed to the response to the director's request for information about the novel's use. Nevertheless, the teacher not only helped to write the explanation of her activities regarding the assignment but also, in so doing, justified her use of the novel.

During our interview Hansen also commented on the reaction of her peers to the book incident:

> I guess I had a lot of support in the schools. Our librarian, Anne Davis, was excellent, just excellent. But there were divisions on the staff, I must say. Some thought that I should have been thrown out on my ear, and some thought that I was doing what I should have done.

However, reaction to the teacher's assignment was not limited to the school setting. After the controversy became public, she began to receive obscene phone calls. The teacher described the calls:

> Heavy breathers and all kinds of things like that. In fact, it got to the point where I had told Arthur [her principal] . . . . And George Roberts [the superintendent] actually called me on the telephone and said, you know, these are some tips for dealing with people who are doing that.

On June 15 the teacher made a presentation at the Supplementary Materials Review Committee meeting. From her point of view, her role as the teacher and that of the parent were antagonistic. She said her plan was not to attack the parent but to defend herself. Her presentation consisted of the information in her letter of June 10. Commenting later on the presentation, Hansen gave her perspective on the purpose of the committee's meeting and her interpretation of the findings. First, she felt that she was being "graded"; second, she felt that the committee members had exonerated her of wrongdoing. Hansen commented:

> I was trying to defend my position, and that's very hard to make the distinction; and very hard to keep yourself on you're defending what you did. You are not attacking, you know. You're not saying, well this — or well, that or all those other things. That I — [pause]. You know, I have heard talk, and I know what's going on in other places. But I didn't bring any of that out. Plus any other things I knew, I didn't bring up. I was only there to defend what I did; I didn't accuse, which is what he did.

The teacher's husband was not allowed to attend the Supplementary Materials Review Committee meeting. While no one source could explain why this occurred (indeed, some said that they didn't realize it had happened), two interviewees confirmed the fact that he was not allowed into the meeting room. The teacher said:

> No, they [the administrators] didn't allow him [to attend]. They said it just had to be me. And, I don't know why I didn't pursue it, but I think I was under the assumption that I didn't want to rock the boat any more than I already rocked the boat. I was trying to keep my cool, trying to show them, you know, my professionalism, that, you know, I could handle and overcome all kinds of obstacles, and still come through [laughs]. You know, I was still looking out for my future, and I wasn't going to rock any boat. If they said he can't come in, fine. . . . They [the parent and his wife] could come together, but maybe that's because they lodged the complaint together, and I'm not really sure if they did. I don't know if the complaint said Mr. and Mrs. But I was there alone. . . . He [the teacher's husband] knew everything. I don't know what — if afraid of what he might add or say, whatever, I don't know. But you were only allowed to speak when you were asked to, so you know, you could not speak up unless you were recognized and allowed to speak.

In spite of her husband being barred from the meeting, the teacher felt that she had a fair chance to present her information. She reported that she was glad to have had the letter that she had sent to the director on June 10. She reported that she presented information and then the parent and his wife presented information. She summarized the experience by stating, "I wasn't there to be put on trial; I wasn't there to put down everything that he was saying."

The teacher also believed that the committee supported her rationale for assigning *Go Ask Alice*. She said:

> I was graded. They [the committee] voted on four different areas. One was — the first one was — was it [*Go Ask Alice*] used appropriately? Uh, and I don't even remember what all the other ones were. One was should a parent letter have gone home? But all the ones that considered myself, all were good. You know, it was used appropriately; was there background material laid? and all these other kinds of things — that was all really good. They said that was great. But they said from now on that a letter should have gone home with the book saying this is what we're doing; and if you disagree, fine, then your child won't be reading it. So that's all that really came out of it, and the books are back on the shelves.

Later in the interview, she described how the committee voted:

> They had four things to vote on, and I can't even remember what all four of the things were. Uh, but they voted three ayes, and one was no. One said what should be from now on is that a parent cover letter goes home with the book saying if they can read it. Did I use it competently? Did I get well-prepared? And there was something else; I can't — I can't even remember. It was all things about me, and they were all good through all the discussion; and in fact, there was only one dissension on the cover letter, and that was Martin Olson [the director]. All of the others were four-zero, four-zero, four-zero. Excuse me, that was three to one. That they still didn't think that the letter was necessary.

After the Supplementary Materials Review Committee meeting ended, the teacher felt relieved that her role in the controversy had been explained and that the reasons behind the assignment had been acceptable to a committee of her peers. Hansen said:

> I was very relieved. The book still wasn't going to be used, and I knew it. I knew if I ever got back in the classroom, they took away a large part of what I could do, but I was happy that it ended the way that it did.

Even though the teacher was satisfied with the findings of the Supplementary Materials Review Committee, the resolution of the last two issues was unsatisfactory to her. First, she was unhappy about the way in which the novel was taken from the students. Second, she knew that because of the protest and the way it occurred, other teachers were going to be intimidated. She said:

> I felt real bad. Well, when they brought in the book — first thing in the morning, students were coming in with high-fives. "Way to go, Mrs. Hansen. We made the paper!" And I'm going, Oh no! They were seriously reading the book before I collected them. Uh, and most of them didn't want to turn them in, but they did. And then the issue of censorship was brought up, but I was told not to discuss it, and I can't remember who told me that. It was somebody up on top. I was not allowed to discuss anything; I was to collect the books and that was it. That was all. No more discussion about anything. . . . I felt that was wrong. We should have at least discussed censorship, and I'm sure what they were looking at was, again, [the student]. You know, she was in that class; and I mean, how, after that, could I judge anything you know in a real objective light when it came to her? Every assignment I gave, everything, I double-checked, and I double-checked and I double-checked. Because I wanted to make sure that this — I could not get caught on it again. And that was really — was not good. It wasn't good for anyone. And it wasn't good that it was squashed, that they weren't allowed to talk about it, weren't allowed to discuss it, that I always had to say, "no comment." And it's making

me look incompetent, as though I did something wrong and, boom, it's taken away and we're not allowed to discuss it any more. These kids are older than that, you know. Maybe you can do that to a little one playing with something they shouldn't and say, 'Cause I say so, that's why. But at this age you can't do that any more. You know, and I think that would've been a good opportunity for them to learn from. But they didn't even give me a chance.

The controversy intimidated both the teacher and her colleagues. She reported that during the next semester:

I didn't give them one piece of literature other than what was in the basal reader. I just couldn't; I — you know — they have taken it — and that was even brought up, that they have taken away — even regular classroom teachers who have been there for years are real hesitant what they were taking off the shelves as a result of this. They still are very hesitant. Because you're just not sure. . . . What I think bothers them most is that he was a fellow teacher, and he knew the rules and procedures. And that's what really bothers them. And I guess that [pause] I don't know, that takes away some of your creativity, you're always thinking, who's looking over my shoulder? And, you know, if a fellow teacher can do this to me, you know, then what's stopping anybody else. I think that they are very hesitant, and I see that; that they are very hesitant.

Also, Hansen reported that she had become very careful about recommending books to the students in her reading class. She said:

I'm real careful. Well, like I said, one of the effects on the kids is that I don't, you know, I don't assign any literature. Another effect it might have on them is that I'm real careful what I do in the classroom. I watch it very closely when they say, I don't know what to read. What's good? And I'm real selective when I even offer them something to read, saying Why don't you try this author? or this author? . . . I make sure all the bases are covered and there's nothing that I could get into trouble for.

Like the parent, the teacher was critical of the media. She felt that only one side of the controversy was being discussed in the media and that the underlying goal of the media was to "sensationalize" the controversy. Although she had been instructed to say, "no comment," she also felt that the newspaper and radio reporters should have attempted to contact her to get her point of view. At the same time, she felt as though the media's interest was, to an extent, an infringement of her privacy. She discussed the media with these words:

> They never used my name, but I'm sure it was brought up somewhere along the line. How did I feel? I felt that they could have at least called me and, you know, Mr. Andrews didn't, but somebody could have said to me, "Gee, do you know what you're in for?" but nobody — Do you know what it's like to listen to the radio in the morning and hear that on the radio as you're driving to school? And, I'm going, Oh, no, should I turn around and go home and call in sick, or what should I do? And I mean it was just all over school; it was just all over immediately; it was so fast. . . . And they didn't — no one at the school was informed of it until we found out about it. Until I heard it on the radio. Never called or anything; and I think that's the least they could have done — to find out some in-depth information. . . . . They didn't give a chance to say anything, or do anything. You know, all you heard was his [the parent's] side, and that I'm passing out pornography, and that was untrue.

CHAPTER SEVEN

THE DIRECTOR

The director of instructional services during the *Go Ask Alice* controversy was Martin Olson. He had held his position with the Newport Area School District for 15 years when the controversy began. During the interviews, other administrators reported that of all of the employees of the school district, the director knew more about the 550 board of education policies than anyone else. Indeed, during the committee work of revising Policies 6144, 6161, and 6163, the director was able to cite direct quotations from original policies and match them with revisions of those policies.

For the most part, the director handled parent protests made about classroom materials as those protests were made, if they were not resolved within the school where the challenge was made. Usually such protests were referred to him by a building principal, either as a result of a unresolved complaint made to a staff member or because a parent contacted the principal directly and was not satisfied with the principal's response. The *Go Ask Alice* protest was the exception.

When asked about the frequency of book protests, Olson said that there had not been an extraordinary number of protests or questions asked before or after the controversy. But there had been a few protests at all levels, elementary through high school:

> probably 50/50 between library books and textbooks. And, uh, very — we have not had any challenges to my knowledge of a textbook after adoption. We have had chal-

77

lenges of supplementary textbooks and of library reading materials. For example, a book of plays used at Washington High School in a dramatics course was challenged. And some elementary and middle school library materials were challenged. To my recollection, we have not had a challenge on an officially adopted textbook.

He also believed that protests should be handled in the building in which they occur. Then, if there is need for further mediation, the protest could work its way to his office and ultimately to the board of education. Indeed, the revised version of Board Policy 6163 reflects just that procedure.

Although Olson was not at the Community Input Meeting of May 5 when the protest was made, he soon became instrumental in developing the official response and resolution to the controversy. Throughout the interviews, the director maintained that the *Go Ask Alice* controversy was part of a continuum. He recalled protests of materials that occurred both before and after the *Go Ask Alice* controversy. He said that the policies that were revised after the controversy were in need of revision before the controversy occurred and would have been revised eventually in any case. Like the superintendent, the director felt that the *Go Ask Alice* controversy was a side issue, a problem not central to the daily running of the school district. He commented:

> One of the things that happens to any public agency is you get side issues. And a side issue can make things look as though you don't have your act together, and people have a lack of confidence in the system. So they can say they're screwing this up. So you do get side issues. If it appears that the organization doesn't have its act together on one issue, it can create doubts on others.

Olson also felt that the public nature of the controversy made it unusual. He explained:

> There have been just as significant book challenges, in my opinion, that did not get into the press at all. And both were handled in a very, uh, probably much the same way.

However one gets a lot more community attention, because it was in a public forum and did get into the *Newport Press*, and because of that, you've got concerns, really, on both sides of the issues. I really had more contact from people who felt the school should have the right to use such books and they should be used, than I got criticisms because we were using the book. In the phone calls that came after the meeting — and when I say more, probably five.

The director cited two more reasons why the *Go Ask Alice* controversy was unusual. First, the method of protest chosen by the parent differed from procedures customarily used by parents who question materials used in classrooms. Second, the superintendent's immediate action of removing the book at a public forum was unusual. From the director's point of view, had both the parent and the superintendent used the correct procedures, the controversy would not have occurred. However, on May 6, he was called to the superintendent's office, briefed on the parent's protest of the book, and given the task of resolving the controversy.

The director's task was difficult for four reasons: 1) The decision to remove *Go Ask Alice* had already been made and had been announced by the superintendent; 2) the director knew that board policies had to be followed or legal problems could occur; 3) he had to try to discover which reading list was being used, and he had to determine if the assignment had been mandatory or voluntary; and 4) he felt that the dual role of the parent, who also was a teacher, complicated the issue in that constitutional rights of free speech and due process were factors in two dimensions — Andrews' rights as a teacher and his rights as a parent.

It was easy for me to trace Olson's efforts in the *Go Ask Alice* controversy because he was the author of many of the documents in the superintendent's file. Furthermore, like the other three key players, he was interested in having his perspective on the controversy known. He was easy to interview because he organized his responses in a way that was thematic and logical.

One important theme emerges from the director's account of the controversy. Olson consistently focused on the internal policies and resources of the district to achieve a resolution, because his job was to develop an "in-house" solution to the problem. This "in-house" solution contrasted with the public solution developed and upheld by the superintendent.

When we discussed the events of the evening of May 5, at various points in our conversation Olson reiterated that he had not attended the meeting and had not been a "firsthand" witness. These were his thoughts about the meeting:

> I was out of the district and did not attend the forum. I think the only unique thing would be that John Andrews, as a professional staff member, would have had other communication channels to use. And he chose not to use them. So he used a rather dramatic presentation to the board of education, a community forum. Now, he was doing it as a parent, and the purpose of the forum is for persons to express concerns to the board. So, certainly it was appropriate. The unusual thing is that he apparently had not discussed it with the language arts staff or with the principal of the building prior to—to discussing it with the forum. And, again, the more usual channel would have been — as a parent — to discuss it with the teacher and the principal. And then, as a professional staff member, and reading people. So I guess the different thing about it was the public forum itself. Most challenges come through first a discussion at the building level.

Olson was aware of possible legal implications regarding the controversy. But it was difficult to understand how he used the concept of due process. In one sense, he implied that due process referred to a correct way of handling the controversy. In another sense, he seemed to suggest that due process was unique to the dual role of the protester, parent/teacher. He said:

> We got into some legal questions with *Go Ask Alice*. The superintendent at the public hearing made kind of a snap judgment. And I'm not sure what his exact words were, but he indicated the books would be removed from the library, or something of that sort. And there were two problems with

that. One, it was not following the procedures in the policies, and the due process. And then, two, would that have been an illegal censorship? So because it was kind of a dramatic setting, and there was that statement, we did have to question, we did have to question the due process, and we didn't want to get into a violation of the First Amendment. So we carefully reviewed the legal steps in due process. . . . And that was the difficulty here. That when the superintendent made a statement in public, we wanted to be sure that his decision was legal, in terms of due process, and in terms of the First Amendment. That's one of the things that complicated this, when John chose not to use the usual channels. Because he did get — though I was not there — I gather he got a rather dramatic response from the audience, and from some board members and the superintendent. And of course, persons want to do something [snaps fingers] there and then some persons do. [laughs] And I was not there, but I gather that some board members wanted some immediate response, and that the superintendent did say something to the effect that the book would be removed. And, it wasn't clear if that meant from the classroom or the library. And too — so we clarified that decision in a written memo to be sure it was clear we were stopping the use in the classroom, but we were keeping it in the library.

The director's memo, dated May 27, began the process of detailing how the book protest would be handled:

A complaint about a book has been referred to me. . . . We are reviewing it per policy 6144, p. 3. Dr. Roberts has directed that the book not be used for instruction in the interim [the time between the protest and the review]. . . . This is not a complaint about a library book under policy 6163. The book need not be removed from the library if it is part of the collection.

Olson's first decision was to use the board policy that deals with controversial issues in supplementary materials, Policy 6144, rather than Policy 6163, which deals with library materials. As detailed in the chronology of the controversy (see Chapter 1), members of the Media Committee had sent a letter to the superintendent, objecting to his action of removing the book and recommending that the controversy be resolved following the guidelines of Policy 6163. Because it wasn't clear (from the director's perspective) whether the superintendent intended to remove the book from both the classrooms and the libraries, and it was clear that the parent had protested the reading of *Go Ask Alice* in a classroom setting, Olson limited the scope of the controversy to supplementary materials used in classrooms. This was a key factor in solving the problem.

Olson stressed the differences between materials found in libraries and materials used for classroom instruction and how those differences were addressed in the school board policies. He explained:

> It's a different selection policy within the school district. And the review procedure was different for supplementary textbooks. That was in the controversial issues policy [6144]. And it says there, complaints come directly to me and my department, and I set up a review committee, which I did. With the library materials, the first complaint goes to the building principal and the building committee. So that is one difference. . . . And then the related question is, who chooses those? For the library books, there's a clear selection policy. For the textbooks, there's a clear selection policy. For the supplementary material, in the policy on controversial issues, it is left to the discretion of the teacher. However, in practice, in some curriculum committees, it has been done by the curriculum committee. For example, in ninth- and tenth-grade English, the curriculum committee selected the novels we use to teach the novel. In the middle school reading program, the supplementary novels were picked in the individual buildings, largely by the reading teacher with input from other teachers. So we have diverse practices on the selection of supplementary materials.

Olson also was aware of legal differences between classroom materials and library materials. He explained:

The difference on library materials and text materials is
— my understanding is legally there is a right for boards of
education and educators to select instructional materials and
eliminate some others. And that is not abridging people's
freedom of the press. Because we select materials to suit our
curriculum and our board policies, which include the curriculum guidelines.

With these distinctions in mind, Olson approached the *Go Ask
Alice* controversy as a curricular matter. He contended that teachers were permitted to choose supplementary materials from any
that were available in order to meet the instructional needs that
they perceived. He commented:

If we choose not to use *Go Ask Alice* to teach about diaries,
that's saying it's an instructional decision on how we're
reaching our organizational goals. And it's different from
saying, we don't want people to read this book. It's a different purpose. It's a different legal question. And I can't cite
you cases. I understand there are some court cases that indicate that school boards and schools do have the legal right to
select instructional materials.

Olson contrasted this position with that of students making
individualized selections from library collections:

Our library collection policy says — it's to suit the needs
of our students, and the needs of the curriculum. So we don't
have to have all possible books in our library. The nature of
a library is to give people choices of materials. And I think
it's more sensitive and more likely to abridge First Amendment rights if you pull something from a library without due
process than from a classroom. . . . And to me it's rational
that if the purpose of supplementary textbooks and textbooks is to deliver an educational program, and you pick
those materials for a different reason than you do the library
materials. The library materials have a similar purpose, to
deliver an educational program; but it's broader, you expect
kids to have choices.

Clearly, Olson was well aware that part of the confusion experienced by the superintendent, the parent, the teacher, and others was caused by the array of policies for different materials, policies for protesting, and policies for removal of materials. These polices were not consistent with one another. To remedy those inconsistencies, he created a Policy Review Committee to coordinate the myriad policies and eliminate some of the confusion. He commented:

> We had diverse challenge procedures. The challenge for a supplementary book came directly to my office. The challenge of library media materials — library media center materials — started at the building level, and then got referred to my office and then to the superintendent. And I felt it would make sense to have consistent challenge procedures. On textbooks, there was really no written challenge procedure.

The director also knew that removal of materials from a library constituted one type of legal issue, while removal of materials from the classroom constituted another. According to the director, to remove materials from a library might abridge First Amendment rights and be seen as censorious. However, he believed that the removal of materials from a classroom would be seen as an educator's professional decision, eliminating materials that were not integral to the instructional program. Conceiving the issue in that way helped Olson to fashion an "in-house," or procedural, resolution of the controversy. By evaluating the book's suitability for instructional use, he side-stepped the issues of profanity and vulgar depictions of sexual conduct that were the original reasons for the parent's protest.

The next major step in achieving an "in-house" resolution to the *Go Ask Alice* controversy was to establish the Supplementary Materials Review Committee, which met on June 15. In preparation for that meeting, Olson sent a memo, dated June 5, to the principal of Lincoln Middle School. In that memo he requested information "on the use of the book in instruction." As recounted previously, he received the requested information on June 9.

Also previous to the committee meeting, Olson contacted the school board's attorney. In a letter dated June 8, he asked the attorney for advice about processing the complaint about *Go Ask Alice*. The letter stated in part:

> We are dealing with a complaint under the enclosed Board of Education Policy 6144, page 3 subparagraph 4. As provided in that policy the complainant has been invited to submit his complaint in person or in written statement. I am also obtaining from the principal information on how the book was used in instruction as it relates to the policy. Copies of memos to the complainant, Arthur Fredericks [Principal, Lincoln Middle School], and the members of the review committee are enclosed for your information. I assume that the review should start with a summary of the policy under which we are functioning, proceed to information about how the book was used in instruction, continue with the complainant's stating his complaints, and then proceed to allowing members of the review committee to ask questions. I assume that I should then ask the members of the committee for their position on whether the book was used appropriately under the policy and whether its use should be continued. I also assume that their positions are advisory to me and that I would make a recommendation to the Superintendent as Director of Instructional Services. Procedures on the policy are not spelled out in any detail. I assume that this is a rather informal procedure, but your advice on good process and potential legal problems is solicited.

One of the interesting elements of the director's letter to the attorney is the assumption that Olson made about the decision of the committee. In the second-to-last paragraph, the director asks the attorney if it is correct to assume that the committee's decision is advisory, and not binding, as the director develops a final decision regarding the use of *Go Ask Alice*. The director was making sure that in setting up a committee to review the use of the novel, he was not relinquishing his power to develop a decision and would not be limited by the committee's actions. The director apparently anticipated that the committee might reach a conclusion that would be difficult to explain to the parent, the public, and the superintendent. Therefore, Olson wanted to maintain control of the final decision that he would pass on to the parent, the superintendent, and ultimately the public.

Olson received two responses from the attorney. During the morning of June 12, the attorney, the coordinator, and the director participated in a conference call regarding the Supplementary Materials Review Committee meeting. They developed a basic agenda and adopted guidelines for processing information. The basic information of the conference call was repeated in a letter from the attorney to the director, dated June 12. Neither the notes from the conference call nor the information from the letter revealed whether the director's assumption about the advisory status of the committee was correct.

The director chaired the Supplementary Materials Review Committee meeting of June 15, during which he reportedly said:

> The book was used appropriately. I am concerned that we have no way to alert parents and students to possible objectionable or controversial issues. I don't think the books should be taught to 12- or 13-year-olds. Such a controversial book may detract from teaching rather than add to it. Some families in the community may object. The book should be in the schools for use with some individuals.

A preliminary draft of the committee's report was written by the coordinator of language arts and reading, David Walker. The preliminary draft was sent to the committee members for approval or suggestions for changes. The director had his own suggestions for changes. Olson sent Walker a memo in which he annotated the decision reached by the Supplementary Materials Review Committee. He wrote in his memo, "I think that the decision should include qualifiers agreed to by the committee." The qualifiers were as follows, with the director's addition in italics:

It is the decision of the committee that the book *Go Ask Alice* should continue to be used in the middle schools *for educational goals that it suits, provided that students and parents are advised of potentially controversial content and alternate materials can be selected by them.*

It is important to note that the director's revision of the committee's statement subtly but specifically changes the committee's finding. The director uses the evaluative elements of "educational goals," "informing of parents," and "alternative assignments" to modify the decision. In its original sense, the committee's decision supported the teacher and did not support the actions of the parent or the superintendent. By his additions, Olson was able to reverse the committee's finding in order to support the parent and the superintendent.

The letter from the director to the superintendent includes a summary of the committee's findings. The amended paragraph from the committee report is included in its entirety. I point this out so that there is no suggestion that the director ignored, overlooked, or intentionally omitted the committee's decision. He simply disagreed with it, and he felt empowered to make a decision contrary to it. Olson's decision to treat the controversy as one about supplementary classroom materials, his question about the advisory status of the committee's findings, the statements he made during the committee's deliberations, and the phrases he added to the committee's decision all were carefully planned.

In his report to the superintendent, Olson summarized the committee's findings, the committee's thinking on the issue of using the book with entire classes, Policy 6144 (which he interpreted as giving him power to develop the decision), and his decision. Olson's wrote:

I find that the book is not appropriate for use as a supplementary text with middle school reading or language arts classes for three reasons. First, the language and controversial content of the book detract from the prime purposes intended — developing literary appreciation, studying the diary format, and learning about characterization. The need to inform students and parents of potentially objectionable language and content and the fact that some students and parents do find them objectionable *per se* detract from the prime goals of reading instruction.

Second, there are other supplementary materials that will suit the prime instructional goals well. *Go Ask Alice* is far from being great literature. There are other books with the diary format that will appeal to the middle school age group and other books that will do a better job with characterization and other literary techniques. Third, there are better media for the secondary purpose for which the book was used, providing opportunities to investigate drug use and abuse. The book is not entirely factual but may appear to be so. Recent news reports of the deaths of youths from drug abuse would be factual and have the same potential emotional impact. Health education teachers and others do use other media for drug education in the middle schools.

In a sense, the director used information Hansen generated for the committee, the report from the middle school principal and the reading consultant, as well as the letter from the teacher and the committee's findings, to justify his result. He also used institutional mechanisms and materials from within the district to develop his solution to the controversy, a solution that was "in house," or procedural.

While two of the Supplementary Materials Review Committee members were appalled by his decision, and members of the Media Committee were outraged, the key players were not. The superintendent felt that the director's decision justified his own actions. The parent was pleased that the book would not be used. The teacher felt that her appearance before the committee had vindicated her actions. And, as reported in the chronology, newspaper accounts of the director's decision did not stimulate much criticism from outside the school system. A subsequent community survey taken by the Language Arts and Reading Evaluation Committee also failed to elicit any criticism of the director's actions.

Although the director did not receive criticism from people outside the school district, many members of the professional staff were upset with his decision. Two staff members were quoted by the *Newport Press* as objecting to the procedures used in reaching the decision and to the withholding of information from students. Some critics even became members of the Policy Review Committee that revised the procedures for protesting the use of books and the handling of such protests. Ironically, it was Olson who created that committee in order to revise the policies to improve their procedural consistency and to prevent someone in his position from having to act again as he had done.

PART THREE
Analysis of the Process

CHAPTER EIGHT

ASSESSMENT: THE RULES AND THE RESULTS

In what respects was the *Go Ask Alice* controversy important to the key players? The answers to this question help frame the discussion of procedures and latent results.

The teacher felt that the controversy had the potential to be career-threatening; it can be inferred that the controversy was of primary importance to her. The parent, also a teacher, was willing to make his arguments about the book in a public forum; the issue clearly was important to him.

On the other hand, both administrators described the controversy as a "side issue," something that detracted attention from their primary responsibilities in the day-to-day operations of the school district. For both the director and the superintendent, the controversy was of secondary importance when measured against their normal responsibilities.

Yet, even for these administrators, "side issue" though it might have been, the controversy introduced important concerns. For the superintendent, the public protest of a book at the open meeting of the board of education implied that he did not have control of the district. In this regard, the controversy was important for reasons of public relations. Furthermore, it was important to the superintendent for him to act quickly so that he could assume responsibility and keep the members of the board of education from acting imprudently. In this respect, too, the controversy amounted to something other than merely a disagreement about what students should read. Thus, for the superintendent, the controversy was focused by political power concerns rather than curriculum concerns.

Although the director also characterized the controversy as a side issue, his involvement in the resolving the controversy actually was greater than the superintendent's. He was required to develop a resolution that satisfied the superintendent, met the requirements of the school board policies, and was legal.

The director processed this book controversy as another of his institutional responsibilities. Because book protests are infrequent, it was a responsibility that he would rarely have to meet. Indeed, the director felt that the occurrence of this controversy was merely part of a continuum. Books had been protested before *Go Ask Alice*, and books would be protested after this controversy was resolved. But the public nature of the protest and the superintendent's decision to remove the book complicated the controversy and distinguished this book protest from others that preceded it.

Both the superintendent and the director knew that procedural (and political) mistakes had been made and that the book protest might have been handled more effectively. I suggest that understanding the latent and manifest elements at work in the institution is a useful — indeed, essential — perspective for assessing how the controversy was handled and what procedures might be used in future book protests in order to avoid repeating the mistakes made during this controversy. These latent and manifest elements can be best examined through two lenses: rules and results.

Latent and Manifest Rules

Manifest rules appear as laws, policies of the board of education, administrative directives, and findings and decisions of committees. Latent rules are unwritten but form a code generally understood by the majority of the staff and, in some cases, by others outside the institution.

The parent's role in the controversy — his actions and the responses they evoked — reveal one set of latent rules. The first such rule is that how a problem is processed is as important as the substance of the problem. There are many subpoints to this rule. First, employees or members of the institution are not supposed to make the internal problems of the institution public. Using a public forum suggests that the institution (in this case the school district) cannot solve its own problems.

Second, as an initial step in solving an internal problem, employees are expected by their peers and their superiors to contact the appropriate personnel of the district. As a fellow employee, the teacher, even though she was a substitute rather than a regular teacher, expected the parent to contact her about his problem with the assignment of *Go Ask Alice*. The building principal also expected the parent to contact him before presenting the protest to the board of education.

Third, if a problem persists after the initial contact is made with peers and immediate supervisors, the institution member is expected to follow the chain of command, taking the problem through ("up") the hierarchy of the institution. However, this subpoint about using the chain of command requires some qualification. While superiors expect subordinates to fulfill their manifest and latent obligations to the institution by proceeding through the hierarchy, the various superiors within the hierarchy are not obligated regarding lower-ranking individuals. For example, none of the key administrators contacted the teacher for information about the assignment. That was left to her direct supervisor, the building principal. Also, the teacher was not invited to participate in the resolution of the controversy, except in the most offhand way.

Another latent rule that became apparent as a result of the parent's actions dealt with assigned readings: Students whose parents object to assigned reading of supplemental texts will be given alternative assignments. This rule was followed when the parent protested the reading of *The Disappearance* and his daughter was given another assignment. However, the parent did not "invoke" this latent rule in the case of *Go Ask Alice.* Instead, he circumvented the direct solution in favor of making his protest public.

A rule that seems obviously manifest also may have latent interpretations and applications. A manifest rule is that when problems occur, the school district's actions should be guided by its policies. That is what most teachers and administrators expect to happen. However, by removing the book from the classroom and from the libraries, the superintendent contradicted the manifest rule because he did not follow the procedures for processing complaints described in the board policies. In fact, some participants in and observers of the controversy suggested that the superintendent intended not to follow policy — until the director informed him of the possibility of litigation over First Amendment issues.

After the controversy had been resolved, the superintendent said that on the night the parent made the protest, he should have referred the protest to the director, who would have been responsible for processing the protest according to school board policies. However, a latent qualification to this rule is that those individuals who are highest in the institutional hierarchy have the greatest latitude for action with regard to heeding, or ignoring, the manifest rules.

A second latent qualification is that the degree of penalty imposed for not following the manifest rules varies with one's position in the institution. The superintendent was not penalized for straying from the formal policies. On the other hand, the teacher, who believed that she had adhered to the policies and followed the procedures expected of her, still considered the controversy to be career-threatening.

As a result of the teacher's role in the controversy, a latent rule might be stated as follows: Teachers should be very careful about using controversial materials because those who have the power in the district — those higher in the hierarchy — may not support the use of controversial materials if such use gives rise to controversy that may threaten or weaken their power.

The interpretation of Policy 6144, developed by the director with assistance from the school district's attorney, helped to disclose another latent rule. This rule is that while a board of education policy may embody a philosophical stance about an issue, the policy is important mainly for the procedures it describes for handling problems. It was interesting to note that Policy 6144 has quite a lengthy introduction that suggests a strong stance on controversial issues. Other than the last sentence, at no time was this section of the policy mentioned, nor were its implications discussed. At the time of the controversy, Policy 6144 said in part:

> -1-Controversial issues are those having one or more answers which are objectionable to a degree to some groups of people. They are issues of current importance. They point up conflicts in cherished interests, beliefs, of affiliations of groups of citizens. They include conflicting views which are held by individuals or groups who disagree on the proposed solutions to important problems recommended by other groups.
>
> -2-Controversial issues are a part of the program of instruction because they help young people to meet and face such questions. They help young people to learn to consider all pertinent factors. They promote fair and many-sided study of conflicting questions. They help young people to develop techniques for considering controversial questions. They provide young people with techniques which they will use habitually in later life. They help pupils to learn how to resist indoctrination and propaganda. They help to free pupils from the assumption that there is only one correct answer. Free discussion of controversial issues is the heart of the democratic promise which pupils must experience. They are intended to help to prepare pupils for intelligent and conscientious participation in democratic social order. . . . Supplementary materials should be selected for the purpose of presenting other points of view and to provide more comprehensive information. Teachers must be free to use their best judgment in their choice of supplementary materials. The individual teacher would be well advised to consider

with the department head, principal, and others in his subject field, the materials he desires to use. Textbooks used should be those approved in accord with the policies of the Board of Education.

The last sentence of this passage from Policy 6144 assumed more importance than the philosophical stance that precedes it. As mentioned earlier, one key question in the controversy was whether *Go Ask Alice* was included on any approved reading list for middle school students. My point is not that the philosophy of 6144 was misinterpreted, but rather that the philosophy was not discussed as a factor in resolving the controversy.

Latent and Manifest Results

The *Go Ask Alice* controversy produced two types of results: latent and manifest. The manifest, or official, results are easy to describe. There are documents to explain them, and the key players confirmed what happened. The director found that the language in *Go Ask Alice* made the novel inappropriate for use in teaching seventh-grade students about literary appreciation, about the diary format, and about characterization. The book was withdrawn from use in the middle school reading program. The book was made available to the students by inclusion in the library collection. The director's memo to the superintendent regarding his decision about the use of the novel was the last official document of the controversy. Neither the parent nor the teacher pursued the matter further.

Although the director felt that the Policy Review Committee would have begun meeting even if there had been no controversy, a secondary effect of the *Go Ask Alice* controversy was to speed up the formation of that committee and to encourage that committee to work out policy problems that became apparent during the book controversy. Consequently, the committee reviewed and revised Policies 6144 "Controversial Issues," 6161 "Instructional Materials," and 6163 "Library Materials." These revisions later were approved by the board of education.

The *Go Ask Alice* controversy seems to have been a singular public event. In the years since the *Go Ask Alice* book protest, no other book challenges in Newport have been as public as this one. The *Go Ask Alice* controversy did not lead to any similar challenges in a public forum with media coverage. That is not to suggest that parents have not brought questions about reading materials to principals and teachers; it is to suggest that other means of handling the challenges have been used. Furthermore, the surveys subsequently conducted by the Language Arts and Reading Evaluation Committee show that the controversy was of little or no sustained importance — at least to the 1,500 people who responded to community surveys.

In short, the manifest results suggest a certain neatness of procedure and finality of decision. However, the latent results seem to be neither neat nor final. Latent results are more difficult to describe because they are unstated and must be inferred from comments and actions. For example, teachers in the middle school appear to have developed a latent interpretation of the director's finding that *Go Ask Alice* was not appropriate for teaching seventh-grade students. The teachers' interpretation is that the novel is not to be used by anyone at any level of the middle school. This interpretation was derived without any written documents, manifest actions, or specific directions. Indeed, according to the manifest results, this interpretation is incorrect. Nevertheless, a latent result of the controversy has been self-censorship regarding the use of the book that extends well beyond the original focus of the controversy.

Process and Substance

Along with manifest results, latent results help to form a holistic picture of the effects of the *Go Ask Alice* controversy. Another way of looking at the manifest and latent dimensions of this book protest and its resolution is to consider the interweaving of process and substance. Two questions were at the heart of the *Go Ask Alice* controversy: 1) What should schools ask students to read? and 2) Who should decide? I would contend that the first question is a matter of substance, because it entails philosophical principles about education, and that the second question is procedural. Much of the effort toward achieving the resolution of this controversy was spent answering the process question; the district was less successful in addressing the substance question.

It seems clear, looking at the controversy's unfolding from a historical vantage point, that the procedures by which the problems generated by the book protest were solved were more important to the members of the school district than the actual substance of the protest. For example, during the interviews, all of the subjects believed that the parent had the right to challenge the use of the book. However, all of the respondents — including the parent — also believed that the protest *should* have begun in a different fashion. The general thought among the respondents was that, in his dual role as parent and teacher, the parent should have known how to protest the use of a book without making the protest a public event.

Furthermore, because the parent made the protest public, the interviewees believed that some unplanned results occurred. For example, some subjects felt that by going to a public forum, the parent was suggesting that there was something wrong with the system — in other words, that if he followed standard internal procedures, his protest might not be satisfactorily addressed. The coordinator of language arts and reading commented:

> It was because what he did has an air about it of washing one's dirty linen in public. Of making the school system look bad for all of us. You know, of kind of announcing to the world, I'm part of the system and it doesn't work.

Another administrator described the latent implications of "going public" in this way:

> When a person who is involved in the organization speaks up, it has the tendency to the average citizen to add credibility to the fact that there may be something wrong, something that shouldn't be. . . .

100

The interview subjects felt the same way about the superintendent's actions. Almost all of them were sympathetic to the situation he faced: a confrontation with a parent about the use of a book that contained offensive language and explicit descriptions of sexual activities. Most subjects believed that the superintendent was "caught off guard," unprepared for such a confrontation from a member of the institution. Thus there was some sympathy for the superintendent's immediate reaction of removing the book. However, after the shock subsided of hearing the excerpts of *Go Ask Alice* read in public, most respondents also wondered why the superintendent didn't defer to policy instead of maintaining his initial stance of removing the book.

One of the librarians summarized the Media Committee's reactions to the withdrawal of the books when she said:

> We [the Media Committee] said, hey, they [the administration] can't do this [ignore policy and withdraw books], 'cause they have set up the rules themselves, and now they're ignoring them. And that was what really upset us, because we said, hey, if they're going to do this now, what are they going to do next time?

Another administrator described the latent effects of the superintendent's actions:

> It always has a kind of maverick effect when the superintendent does stuff like that. [laughs] You know, superintendents have a tendency to see themselves as, you know, kind of God over the school system, and to some extent that's good because you need a superintendent that's not afraid to take a strong stand or take a role. But, that doesn't mean they are always right. And when they do that, they're gonna end up stepping on some toes periodically.

Some evidence suggests that the superintendent's exercise of power beyond the school board policies served as a model for other administrators in the district. For example, a high school librarian reported that even though the superintendent had not directed the high school librarian to remove *Go Ask Alice*, the book often

101

was missing from its place on the shelves. She said that she would find the book on top of the stacks or behind other books. While she didn't know who was moving the books (it might have been students), she did report a confrontation with an assistant principal over a sign on the wall of her office. The sign said, "I read banned books." She was told to take the sign down because it was a "slap in the face" for the superintendent. The librarian reported:

> He said it was inappropriate. And I said, "Why, why is it inappropriate? . . . The dictionary is one of the banned books." And he said, "I'm not going to argue with you, take it down."

When the assistant principal's demands became known to the faculty of the high school, buttons that said, "I read banned books," were printed and worn during the school day by some of the staff members. And so, although the controversy centered on one of the district's three middle schools, one of the two high schools also was affected.

The director also faced his share of controversy. Although the director's decisions were based on school board policy, his actions were questioned, too. For example, the Media Committee felt that he had chosen the wrong policy, 6144, for reviewing the novel, and, by not reviewing 6163, he was not responding to the fact that the books had been removed from the libraries. Later, after the director had made his decision resolving the controversy, two members of the Supplementary Materials Review Committee felt that their time and effort had been wasted because the director "ignored" the findings of the committee and reached a different conclusion.

Apart from being told to collect the books and not to comment about the controversy, the teacher was left out of the procedures. She was bypassed by the parent who went to the board of education with his problem. Neither the superintendent nor the director contacted her for information regarding the assignment or the intended use of the novel. Thus the teacher, on advice from her lawyer, was compelled to insert herself into the procedures by writing a letter that explained the assignment and its intended outcomes. Later, at the meeting of the Supplementary Materials Review Committee (to which she was only offhandedly invited), she presented her rationale for using *Go Ask Alice*.

The findings of the Supplementary Materials Review Committee suggest that the committee members' interests were more procedural than substantial. They found that the teacher had developed a workable plan. Even though they felt that she should have made the parents aware of the controversial elements of the novel, they found that she had followed correct procedures in developing the lesson and choosing the novel. Because an alternative reading assignment would have been given to students who requested it, they felt that the planned use of the book was appropriate. The committee did not address the first question — What should schools ask students to read? — which would have led them to deal with substance. Instead, they concentrated on the process of selecting and assigning the book and agreed that the correct procedure was used.

The question of substance was partially addressed only by the parent who protested the book's use. However, he never explained what effect he thought the reading of *Go Ask Alice* might have on students. He assumed that the negative effects of reading the novel were apparent, and that those effects justified removing the book from use. No one challenged him to explain his reasoning; he was challenged only on the basis of the procedure he used to accomplish the removal of the book.

A close analysis of the final report sent by the director to the superintendent reveals that the director's findings also are thin on substance. The director wrote:

> I find that the book is not appropriate for use as a supplementary text with middle school reading or language arts classes. . . . First, the language and controversial content of the book detract from the prime purposes intended — developing literary appreciation, studying the diary format, and

learning about characterization. . . . Objectionable language and content . . . detract from the prime goals of reading instruction.

Second, there are other supplementary materials that will suit the prime instructional goals well. *Go Ask Alice* is far from being great literature. . . .

The concepts set out in this finding — "appropriate," "prime reading goals," "literary appreciation," and "great literature" — are difficult to define. But it would not be fair to suggest that in writing this memo the director was attempting to accomplish a philosophical purpose. Rather, the director's implicit purpose was to avoid a legal entanglement. The director used the instruction point of view in order to find the book unacceptable as a teaching tool, thereby avoiding the stickier issue of obscenity. Trying to resolve the controversy by defining obscenity, community standards, and related issues would have led the district into a morass.

Nothing of substance can be found in the director's decision that might assist in the resolution of future book protests. What is great literature? How does great literature differ from literature that is not great? Why isn't *Go Ask Alice* great literature? Who determines which literature is great and which is not great? Should only great literature be read by students? What happens to students who don't read great literature? Questions such as these also might be asked about "literary appreciation," "prime reading goals," and "appropriate." The lack of answers to such questions means that no foundation was laid for dealing with future book protests on similar grounds.

CHAPTER NINE

INSTITUTIONAL VALUES AND PROBLEM SOLVING

Fundamentally, *Anatomy of a Book Controversy* is about a problem and its solution. But no anatomy can be fully revealed merely by studying the problem's surface features. An "internal" examination of how a school district processes a book controversy can reveal some of the basic values that lie at the heart of the institution. Thus revealed, these values can be examined as components in change or reform.

Defining the Problem

The first step in solving any problem successfully is clearly defining the problem, or set of problems. Few problems involving book protests are as simple and straightforward as they may seem initially.

At first, the *Go Ask Alice* controversy seemed straightforward. A parent objected to the reading of a novel. The solution to that problem was the removal of the book. That was the perception at the Community Input Session. However, as the problem and this "quick and easy" solution were examined from various points of view at a reflective distance, the problem and this solution spawned several other problems in need of solutions. Thus the complications of policy interpretation, committee actions, constitutional rights, and expectations contained in latent policies became factors in the later, revised and elaborated resolution of the controversy.

The complexity of a problem in an institutional setting arises from several factors. One factor is perception. The chronological description, complemented by accounts representing the viewpoints of the primary participants — the parent, the superintendent, the director, and the teacher — illustrates various perceptions of the same incident. The superintendent and the director viewed the controversy as a side issue, a distraction rather than a serious problem. But it was a serious problem from the viewpoint of the parent, as the book protest arose from an issue of conscience. It also was a serious problem from the teacher's perspective; in fact, she considered the incident to be career-threatening.

Another factor that complicates problem definition is that the substantive conflicts that give rise to the problem may be especially difficult to define. Moreover, conflicting definitions may create additional problems. In resolving the *Go Ask Alice* controversy, for example, little real effort was made to define the problem substantively. Instead of developing a cohesive institutional response involving the development of consensus among individuals holding various viewpoints, a simpler — albeit, sanctioned — definition was put forward. When the Supplementary Materials Review Committee could not agree on the appropriateness of *Go Ask Alice* as a novel for seventh-grade readers, it became apparent to the director that the easiest way to resolve the controversy would be to rely on procedures. Therefore, the director unilaterally decided that the book was inappropriate for instructional purposes. He then justified his decision using laws and policies that permitted him to make that decision, which essentially disregarded any advice of the committee. By so doing, he was able to turn to a procedural solution based on *his* definition of the problem.

Extraneous or illogical factors also may be introduced to intentionally or unintentionally confuse the process of defining the problem. A simple example from the *Go Ask Alice* controversy occurred at the outset, during the parent's protest. A member of the audience at the Community Input Session reported that the parent prefaced his remarks about the book by addressing the superintendent with the question, "Are you aware that . . . ?" Then the parent went on to read excerpts from the book. In the observer's opinion, the parent was intentionally baiting the superintendent, because the parent then also concluded his remarks with a final question: "What are *you* going to do about it?"

The tenor of these questions — apart from their substance — created a dilemma for the superintendent. If he were to indicate that he was aware of the use of the novel and of its language and descriptions, then he would seem to admit some tacit responsibility for the book's use. On the other hand, if he were to acknowledge that he was not aware, then he would seem to admit irresponsibility because the implication would be drawn that, had he been as responsible as he should have been, the book would not have been used. Thoughtful observers will recognize that it is not possible for the superintendent (or anyone else) to know what is being discussed or assigned in every classroom of the district at any one time. Yet the immediacy of the problem was heightened by the parent's accusatory tone, which urged the superintendent to respond immediately — spontaneously — in order to escape either implication by a quick, decisive action, however impulsively "wrong" it might be judged in retrospect. Thus the superintendent's initial solution to the problem was tactical rather than substantive.

The public relations implications of the problem and its solution overshadowed more substantive issues. This situation frequently occurs when controversies arise in public institutions. The consequence in this instance was that no one took the time to conduct a scholarly analysis of the effects that reading has on students' values. By not extending the discussion to the effect of the book on students, participants responsible for the district's response overlooked an important substantive dimension in defining the problem. Both the parent and superintendent *assumed* that *Go Ask Alice* would affect the students negatively; therefore, the parent wanted the book taken away from all the students, and the superintendent (initially) complied.

The Supplementary Materials Review Committee also concerned itself with procedure, rather than substance. The committee examined whether the book was used correctly and whether it should continue to be used. The committee did not consider the intrinsic merits of this book or similar books or more fundamental issues of curriculum. The parent, in making his public protest as well as in making his argument to the Supplementary Materials Review Committee, simply read excerpts from *Go Ask Alice* that used profane language or detailed sex acts. During the *Go Ask Alice* controversy, everyone avoided asking — or no one thought to ask — how reading a novel like *Go Ask Alice* affects the students.

Such questions seem critical to understanding the substance of the controversy. If anyone had looked, he or she would have found research that might have helped to resolve the controversy, or might at least have provided new information to elaborate the director's purely procedural decision regarding the use of *Go Ask Alice*. For example, Neuman (1986) compared assumptions about the effects of reading on student values with the research that describes such effects. There are three basic findings in Neuman's study. First, she found that reading seems to reinforce opinions, values, and beliefs already held by the reader. Second, she suggested that reading involves a complex interplay between the reader and what is read; therefore, the effect of the material also is complex and varies with each reader. And so predictions as to the reader's response are questionable. Third, Neuman found that the readers' opinions are more likely to be determined by their environment, family, peers, and schooling than by reading alone.

Solving the Problem

The failure to look beyond the immediate and the superficial in terms of defining the problem led to a distorted definition and, consequently, to a distorted solution.

As is true of defining a problem, solving a problem can be more complex than it appears, either initially or in retrospect. The

108

processes used in solving the problem of the *Go Ask Alice* book protest are — or should be — as important to the Newport district as the substance of the problem. Indeed, the solution processes used in many institutional settings take on a significance that is independent from the results they are expected to produce.

In the *Go Ask Alice* controversy, many of the solution processes were ritualistic. By "ritualistic," I mean that the processes followed established formulas: Take this specific step and a predictable result will be achieved. For example, open forums, such as the Community Input Session, can be described as rituals in which citizens bypass the institutional hierarchy and directly address their concerns to the board of education. Even though many people participate in the forum ritual, little action is taken — or expected. Indeed, the parent expressed surprise at the quick response given to him by the superintendent, " 'cause usually at those input sessions, they never make decisions."

Another ritual derives from the school board policies. Many board policies express a philosophical basis and provide a set of procedures for implementing that philosophy. In this case, for example, the application of the procedures found in Policy 6144 was an important step in completing the ritual of policy review and achieving the intended solution. But no one seriously considered the philosophy undergirding the policy or any contrary implications of that philosophy, which might have led to a solution other than the intended one. Ritual demanded that the policy be followed, not questioned.

Similarly, the formation of the review committee to apply the procedures outlined in the policy also was ritualistic. Superficially, the development of committees to help find solutions to problems is a common practice in education. However, in this case, the committee's efforts were neutralized. In essence, the development of a committee was ritualistic, as it gave the appearance of peer review and consensus of opinion. But neither the peer review nor the consensus of opinion was significant in the solution of the problem. The true power to resolve the controversy was vested in the director, who ignored the committee's advice. And the director's solution was supported by the superintendent.

Ritualistic problem solving avoids addressing the deeper causes of problems. Thus, when ritualistic methods are used to solve problems, the solutions tend to be insubstantial or, at best, short-sighted. In the *Go Ask Alice* controversy the solution was reactive, not preventive. Framed by the procedures in Policy 6144, the solution resolved that book protest, but it did not go further. For example, it did not result in the development guidelines for book selection or book evaluation — guidelines that might prevent the same type of protest from developing in the future.

The *Go Ask Alice* controversy also came about because the Newport middle school philosophy was incompletely articulated and only partially realized in policy and day-to-day procedures. The element of selection guidelines illustrates this flaw. In his memo to the superintendent regarding his decision about the use of *Go Ask Alice*, the director recognized that reading lists and criteria needed to be developed. However, his rationale was procedural rather than substantial. He wrote:

> Supplementary book lists for the middle school reading programs have not been established. They should be established by a building committee to suit the instructional goals of the middle school reading program. The supplementary reading lists in the district-adopted Houghton Mifflin reading program should provide a starting point for the committees and serve as the list until they complete their work. The middle school principals should appoint the committees and may have recommendations reviewed by parent advisory committees. D. Jones will advise the committees, provide them with reading lists from the NCTE [National Council of Teachers of English] and other sources, and help to coordinate the middle school and high school reading lists.

No doubt the development of reading lists does require a prescription. But if the district merely emphasizes how the book list is to be assembled without discussing the purposes to be served by such a list, then the district gives up a fundamental element of its curricular authority. As a result, if the district finds itself relying on ritualized methods of solving problems, it will render itself vulnerable to criticism by those who do have strong philosophical stances. In such a conflict the district will have no clear philosophical position from which to counter the criticism.

Assessing Philosophies and Their Implementation

Institutions that hold and clearly articulate a cohesive, comprehensive philosophy will be more successful in solving problems than those institutions that merely follow ritualistic procedures without a clear understanding of the philosophy underlying those procedures. Indeed, without a coherent, commonly held, and commonly understood philosophy, the institution risks promulgating conflicting procedures that create more problems than they solve.

Duck (1981) suggests that various formulations of educational purposes derive from four basic units. The four units are the learner, the subject matter, use of the subject matter, and behavior complementary to the philosophical position. Duck intends to help teachers evaluate their positions and actions by understanding the personal assumptions that guide their decisions as they teach. He refers to his categories as analytical tools and has developed a continuum for each category. At the ends of each continuum are extreme positions. Teachers (and administrators in this case) should find themselves somewhere between the extremes. Duck's categories will serve here to help describe the differences among the key players in the *Go Ask Alice* controversy.

Duck's first consideration is the learner. The question he asks is, "What is the nature of the learner?" One end of the response continuum is labeled *Lockean*, the other *Platonic*. According to Duck, the Lockean perspective suggests that sensory data are absorbed by the learner and that such data form the true source of knowledge. A Platonic viewpoint suggests that the learner gains knowledge through inquiry and interaction with the learning environment, not through passive receipt of information from it.

111

The two key administrators in the *Go Ask Alice* controversy leaned more toward the Lockean than the Platonic position. Both believed that the book contained information that they did not want the Newport schools to be responsible for introducing to students. For example, the profane language was of particular importance to the administrators. As shown earlier in this report, both the superintendent and director cited the book's profane language as having negative curricular value as learners study literature.

The parent and the teacher leaned more toward the middle of the continuum, maybe even toward the Platonic position. The parent asked, "How do you explain, for example, when she [the main character in *Go Ask Alice*] says, 'Then Frank and I went on and had a blow job'?" In short, he wanted not only to prevent the dissemination of such information, but also to prevent interaction between the teacher and students (or the students with each other) regarding the offensive text. The teacher's plans for use of the book showed that she had a variety of learning goals for the students. One of the major goals was discussion or interaction.

Duck's second category has to do with the subject matter. The question he asks is, "What is the nature of the subject matter?" In developing a response continuum, Duck uses *amorphous* and *structured* student responses to subject matter as the extremes. Amorphous means "the ability to repeat items and details, without any corresponding capacity to demonstrate insights about the relationships among separate items" (p. 7). Structured means "having a natural structure which can help to explain relationships among its components which can also be used to find out new information within the subject matter" (p. 9).

When assessing the actions of the administrators, the parent, and the teacher in regard to this continuum, it is hard to find differences. None of them felt that the students' reaction to the material in *Go Ask Alice* would be amorphous. All of them recognized that there was some structure to the book and that in presenting the book to the students, the teacher would cover a variety of different topics that were related to one another.

The third category describes the use of the material. Duck's question is, "How should one use the subject matter to guide students toward meaningful learning activities?" At the end points of this continuum, Duck has placed the words *affective* and *cognitive*. In the cognitive domain are facts, concepts, and generalizations. In the affective domain are beliefs and values.

This category seems to describe the core of the *Go Ask Alice* controversy. The teacher believed that she had selected a book that would emphasize certain facts, concepts, and generalizations. In contrast, the parent believed that this same book threatened his values. As the data collected for this study were evaluated, it became clear that the key players' actions were based on their conflicting beliefs. For instance, the parent was afraid that the cognitive elements of the assignment would be overshadowed by the affective elements, or the beliefs and values inherent to the telling of the story. The superintendent said that he acted to remove the book because he wanted to demonstrate the values held by the school district. He, too, was concerned about the affective effect of reading the book, and he was worried about the general perception that the public might form about the values of the school district.

The director held another point of view. He justified the removal of the book because he thought that profane language made it inappropriate for use in teaching other objective concepts, such as the diary technique and characterization. The teacher had chosen the book, in part, because it seemed to be material that the students could read and evaluate in terms of the diary format and characterization. She also felt that she had chosen a book that was relevant to a social issue, drug abuse; and she hoped her use of the book would have some affective results on students' views of that issue.

On Duck's third continuum, the director would be placed toward the cognitive end. The superintendent and the parent would be placed toward the affective end. And the teacher would be toward the middle. These distinctions, therefore, reveal much of the true nature of the controversy and offer a perspective on the various players' actions.

Duck's final category deals with classroom behaviors complementary to a philosophical position. On one end of this continuum is the authoritarian world view. Authoritarianism involves convergent thinking, or thinking aimed at convergence on the one correct answer. Non-authoritarian or divergent thinking marks the other end point. Divergent thinking seeks out many responses to questions.

One reason the *Go Ask Alice* controversy developed was that the parent and the superintendent felt that there was one correct way to view the use of the book, and that way was negative. On the other hand, the director and the teacher held different opinions. If the question were asked, "Is *Go Ask Alice* a good novel for teaching about the diary technique of writing and the study of characterization?" the director would say no. But the teacher would probably say yes (although it must be recalled that the teacher also chose the book for practical reasons of availability and quantity). If the question were, "Is *Go Ask Alice* a good novel?" the superintendent, the director, and the parent would say no. The teacher would say yes. If the question were, "Should *Go Ask Alice* be used in the school district?" the superintendent and parent would say no, and the director and teacher would say yes.

The question that Duck posed for this category was, "What behavior pattern should one exhibit in order to carry out one's philosophical position?" The superintendent and parent fit close to the authoritarian end of the continuum. They both felt that the book would have the same negative effect on all of the students. Their behavior patterns indicate an authoritarian stance. The superintendent, who decided on immediate removal of the book from classrooms and libraries, was the most authoritarian. The parent, who decided that the book would not be read by his daughter — and should not be read by other students — also acted in an authoritarian manner. The director, who decided that the book was inappropriate, was not as superficially authoritarian as the parent or the superintendent. The director did go through the procedures for gathering information and basing his decision on that information. However, eventually, he also took an authoritarian stance by arriving at a solution contrary to the advice of the review committee. The teacher clearly was the least authoritarian of the group. She had multiple reasons for choosing the book and multiple goals for the students to meet.

Duck also proposes two broad continua that draw on the elements of the previous four, based on how those questions are answered. One of these illustrates the nature of the curriculum (or how key individuals believe the curriculum should be structured), and another illustrates a broad philosophical stance (or how these individuals view the nature of education).

In terms of curriculum, the end points are *most structured* and *least structured*. Applying the information from the previous categories, it would be fair to place the superintendent, the parent, and the director toward the *most structured* end of the continuum. The teacher would fall somewhere between these three individuals and the *least structured* end of the continuum.

In terms of philosophy, Duck proposes two broad categories: *perennialist/essentialist* and *experimentalist/existentialist*. The first category, Duck says, is supported by stimulus/response theories of learning. Duck associates it with the use of behavioral objectives and with the assumption that a question has one correct answer. The experimentalist/existentialist group is supported by gestalt theories of learning, maintaining both cognitive and affective objectives in teaching. For educators in this latter group, questions may have more than one answer. Limited to these two categories to describe the key players in this controversy, it would be reasonable to suggest that the superintendent, parent, and director are more perennialist/essentialist; the teacher is more experimentalist/existentialist.

Duck's categories highlight the ways that personnel in a school district may exhibit differing philosophies regarding the learner, what is learned, how what is learned should be taught, and how the educator should enact a philosophical viewpoint. The differences among the Newport personnel are not surprising. It is unlikely that the personnel of any school district would demonstrate only a single educational philosophy. Nor is it likely that any person within a district would hold consistently to the same philosophical position on all matters. In the case of Newport, then, it is understandable that the parties involved attended mainly to process aspects of the *Go Ask Alice* problem. The processes seemed to be far less complicated than addressing the underlying philosophies.

However, the unfortunate consequence of emphasizing only processes is that rituals develop, and these rituals embody philosophies of their own. One such "independent" philosophy might be described as *traditional* or "we've always done it that way." Chances for change within an institution are minimized when rituals become entrenched.

Stasis Versus Change

According to Besag and Nelson (1984), institutions typically resist change:

> By its nature and establishment, an institution becomes self-justifying and reluctant to make dramatic alterations. There is a status quo orientation in an institution that is difficult to overcome. The institution was established for certain social purposes, has survived by doing things in certain ways, and the actors fear major disruption in that process. An institution tends to be conservative and self-protective. (p. 37)

From the viewpoint of the institution, the resolution to the *Go Ask Alice* controversy may be the best that could have been developed. Manifest effects were minimal; consequently, the school district did not have to accommodate any extreme changes.

Reliance on ritualized procedures to solve problems enables the institution to maintain the status quo. This is how it worked in the *Go Ask Alice* controversy. After the controversy, both the parent and the superintendent felt that the parent could have processed his challenge differently and would do so next time. The director orchestrated the revision of three important district policies so that the *processes* they outline are now consistent. Most pre-existing latent rules and underlying philosophies remained intact. The teacher — who worried that the book protest might be career-threatening — now has a full-time job. The only important manifest change has been simply that *Go Ask Alice* is no longer used in the seventh-grade reading program. The book still can be checked out of the school library.

CHAPTER TEN

THE ROLE OF THE SCHOOL IN SOCIETY

The experiences of the *Go Ask Alice* controversy may be useful in broader ways than simply the processing of future book protests. I have proceeded from a view of the institution, according to the terms provided by Besag and Nelson (1984), as "any construct, organization, beliefs, or being that has become identified with an historically expected set of purposes and behaviors." This study of the *Go Ask Alice* controversy disclosed many differences in philosophy, process, and intention by the players as the controversy was processed by the institution. Those differences — how those individuals and others inside and outside the institution view the institution and their roles in it — affect the role of the school in society.

For example, the tension created by the various views of the controversy — a side issue for the superintendent, career-threatening for the teacher — is representative of that general tension that seems to be intrinsic in superordinate-subordinate relationships. That same tension is mirrored in the responses to the controversy. The solutions to the problem that were acceptable to teachers proved to be unacceptable to administrators, and vice versa. At root, these tension-producing differences exemplify a broader difference in how the teachers and administrators view the role of the school (in particular its educative function) in society.

Greenstone and Peterson (1983) described the administrator-teacher (superordinate-subordinate) tension as a product of the dichotomy of functions within the institution of the school. They suggest that until this dichotomy of functions is understood, education reform — or even less extensive problem solving — will not be wholly effective.

Greenstone and Peterson also suggest that educators have two professional roles. One is oriented toward the academic work of maintaining a cultural heritage of intellectualism. This work is done by teaching students methods of inquiry and evaluation and encouraging them to apply those methods throughout their lives. The content for such a curriculum should include basic facts, processes, and skills that can be broadly applied as students progress to more complex tasks. According to Greenstone and Peterson, the teacher's function as promoter of inquiry is best developed when the teacher has freedom and autonomy in the classroom. Without freedom and autonomy, the teacher cannot use personal attributes of insight, expertise, and experience to make instructional adjustments in order to meet the needs of the variety of students. If the classroom teacher has freedom and autonomy, less control can be exercised by superiors and parents.

Greenstone and Peterson suggest that the educator's other role is that of social functionalist. While Greenstone and Peterson assign this role primarily to the administrative side of the education institution, the classroom teacher also is expected to enact this role. The social functionalist has to meet the requirements of constitutional law, state policies, and directives of the board of education. The social functional role is also political in that as an educator enacts the role, he or she is recognizing a responsibility to the community that surrounds and maintains the school. Furthermore, as a social functionalist, the educator responds to the interests and perceived needs of those people. In short, the issue of social control in matters of curriculum and instruction is focused away from the teacher (as promoter of inquiry) and coordinated by superiors, parents, students, and social reformers. Greenstone and Peterson state that "the social functional view is concerned with protecting the rights and satisfying the preferences of individuals within a community of interest" (p. 410).

While it may be argued that educators, both teachers and administrators, have many more roles, this dichotomy of social functionalist and promoter of inquiry aptly describes the philosophical stances underlying the actions taken in the *Go Ask Alice* controversy. But it is important to note that while the dichotomous roles apply here specifically to one teacher and two administrators, that does not mean that all administrators are of one group and all teachers are of another. Nor does it suggest that teachers or administrators act out only a single role all of the time, or that one role is better or more important than the other.

The teacher saw herself as presenting the students with fundamental skills of literary appreciation: understanding characterization and the uses of the diary technique in literature. One of her goals was "to provide students with thinking and skill experiences using information needed to make sound judgments." Thus the teacher was enacting what Greenstone and Peterson call the "promoter of inquiry" role.

By contrast, it seems accurate to describe the superintendent's action during the controversy in terms of the social functionalist perspective. During one of my interviews with him, the superintendent said he sensed that the audience was upset by the parent's reading of excerpts from *Go Ask Alice*. He also said that he often met with civic groups and with the clergy, and consequently he felt that his action of removing the book would receive support from people in the community.

Taken to a higher level, if the question were posed, What is the role of the school in society? the administrative answer would advance the social functional view: The school is responsible to the needs and interests of the community it serves. The teacher's answer would stand on a different philosophical ground: The school should provide basic knowledge, which includes inquiry and application of new information.

Therefore, from the view of Greenstone and Peterson, this basic difference of philosophy underlies the fundamental tension between administrators and teachers. While this view is not absolute, the dichotomy is typical and clearly exemplified in controversies such as the book protest in this case. The particular relevance of the Greenstone and Peterson assertion to this report is that the resolution of the *Go Ask Alice* controversy was developed without any acknowledgment that competing philosophies about the purposes of education or the role of the school were part of the controversy. This omission suggests two consequences. First, the problems presented in the controversy will reappear because the core problem was not addressed. Second, the dominant social functionalist philosophy in the district will provide a limited perspective from which to work in new cases. Both roles — the inquiry and the social functional role — must be taken into account by any district seeking a more satisfactory and long-lasting outcome.

Extending the Lessons of *Go Ask Alice*

Process and substance also are important variables in a more global discussion of how institution members frame problems and develop solutions. Neil Postman offers a more expansive perspective from which the *Go Ask Alice* controversy can be described, and Bill Moyers offers some unusual commentary.

In *Amusing Ourselves to Death*, Postman argues that "the clearest way to see a culture is to attend to its tools for conversation" (1985, p. 8). In making this argument, Postman is revisiting Marshall McLuhan, who coined the phrase, "the medium is the message." Further, Postman credits Plato with the notion that "forms of public discourse regulate and even dictate what kind of content can issue from such forms" (p. 6).

Postman catalogues "the dissolution of public discourse in America and its dissolution into show business" (p. 5). It is Postman's contention that the epistemology of our culture can be described more accurately by examining the visual images that we generate than by examining the written or oral language used to discuss and describe that epistemology. Postman uses the word "epistemology" in its most general sense to mean what we know and how we know it. In this sense "epistemology" describes the way people think about things by framing ideas, asking questions, and developing answers. Postman argues that because of the influence of the media, particularly television, we have reframed our cultural epistemology from the linear-language format to the impressionism of visual imagery.

Postman contends that such reframing of our cultural epistemology causes us to lose language skills of discourse, such as logic and rationalism. Instead, we react to images, and our reactions often are neither logical nor rational. For example, which has more impact, a picture of a protester destroying the American flag or a discussion of the protester's right to make a statement by such destruction? Postman contends that the power of a visual image, such as a protester destroying the American flag, has such an impact that the discussion of the right to make such a statement seems unnecessary and, unfortunately, may never take place.

A second argument made by Postman is that when a language-based epistemology is changed to an image-based epistemology, the description of our world and the framework from which we view it becomes fragmented and lacks cohesion. One of the reasons for fragmentation is the way in which information is presented. For example, much of the information we get today comes from television news shows. News shows incorporate words with pictures. The sound-bite reporting of television fragments the discussion of important topics. Postman contends that pictures dictate how many and in what manner the words are used. Furthermore, the significance of a topic in terms of development of discussion is circumscribed by the picture. Consequently, discourse is limited to the words that describe an image, rather than discuss it.

The Power of Images

Viewing the *Go Ask Alice* controversy from the perspective of image-making and image-maintaining, rather than as a debate of substance, produces several important insights. Postman argues that, because of the proliferation of images and the effect that this proliferation has on our epistemologies, most people accept imagery because they do not want to take the time or expend the energy on analytical discourse about the images. While it may seem impossible to unravel all of the implications of a given image, some images should be unraveled because doing so may be important to understanding the philosophies and motivations of the image makers. Such understanding may be used to meaningfully shape future actions.

Two primary images were generated at the outset of the *Go Ask Alice* controversy. First, the parent created an image of a father protecting his child. Second, the superintendent created an image of action and decisiveness. Both images were powerful enough to confound the answering of the basic questions: What should students read and who should decide what students read?

Picture a father confronting a group of education leaders and questioning them about assigning a book for his daughter to read that contains profane language and is sexually explicit. This image is packed with sociological, psychological, philosophical issues that overwhelm the observer. The immediate effect of this powerful "parent image" as the parent read from *Go Ask Alice* was to move the superintendent to respond — to take action — in order to counteract the image, rather than to explore the issues.

A vast body of literature has been written about the constitutional implications of "freedom of speech" and "due process" embedded in a book protest. However, the "parent image" wiped away all the considerations of constitutional law, all the guidelines from state laws, and all the policies which governed the school district. Instead of turning, reasonably, to these sources for guidance in solving the problem — the challenge to the school's educative decision — the superintendent instead created another image.

To counter what he perceived as the most important implications of the "parent image," the superintendent constructed a decisive "leader image." "That book will be gone," he said. By so doing, the superintendent also overwhelmed the issues. The

124

power of the "leader image" subverted any movement toward rational discourse. In approximately two minutes, the potential for healthy discussion about important, rather fundamental education issues was eliminated.

The parent was surprised by the action of the superintendent. The parent thought that his complaint would result in no immediate action. In fact, he expected to be shunted back to the building principal for further action. Viewed from the image-making/ image-maintaining perspective, the parent expected a rational response to his powerful "parent image." What he got was a counter-image of equal — perhaps greater — power.

When the parent realized the effect of his own image-making, he did two things. First, he refused to be the spokesperson or image-maker for other protest groups. Second, he made himself available to the district administration for further discussion. He wanted to encourage the rational response that he had anticipated. And, indeed, two discussions occurred. However, neither discussion concerned which books should be read or who should decide. Instead, the discussions focused on procedures and using proper channels within the institution. Thus the anticipated rational dialogue never took place.

The superintendent recognized that his actions created an image of leadership. He knew that his action — ordering removal of the book — would anger many people. What is perhaps most telling about the superintendent's understanding of his own image-making is that he chose which people to anger. He chose to anger teachers and administrators, over whom he could exert control, rather than anger people who are outside the institution and over whom he had no control. This choice is logical, and many leaders regard such choices as their prerogative. However, creating a "leader image" at the sacrifice of rational discourse about a controversial issue is an act that confounds the problem and injures the members of the institution.

Of all the members of the institution, the teacher was most affected by the superintendent's action. When the superintendent vowed to act decisively, he implied that the teacher was at fault. She was rendered powerless. She was given no forum for discussion nor opportunity to create an image of her own, a "responsible teacher image," if you will. In fact, her professional role in the institution's processing of the controversy was reduced to the clerical work of collecting the copies of *Go Ask Alice*. She was told not to talk to the media. She was told not to discuss collecting the books or terminating the assignment with her students.

In light of image strategies, perhaps the most useful role was played by the director. By giving the task of solving the book protest problem to the director, I would argue that the superintendent, in fact, gave the director the task of unraveling his "leader image" of forceful action and unraveling the "parent image" of the aggrieved father in order to find elements in each that would lead to rational discourse and a workable solution. Thus the director tried to focus on the legal and policy aspects of the controversy. He gathered evidence. He set up a committee to evaluate the book's use according to board policies. And so on.

In spite of all his efforts, the director was a captive to the power of the images. He could not — or did not — focus on the questions of what students should read or who should decide what they read. As a result, the eventual decision that the book would be removed from the seventh-grade program essentially reflected the power of the images made by the parent and superintendent — and justifications for their actions — rather than conclusions reached after discourse about the substance of the controversy.

The institutional effects of the superintendent's choice of image over discourse illustrate Postman's argument that image-based epistemologies fragment issues and eliminate cohesiveness. When controversial issues are not addressed within a rational framework of policies, interpretations, and substantive dialogue, then confusion erupts among the members of the institution. In the *Go Ask Alice* controversy, teachers and librarians were angry and administrators were confused because they all were asked to uphold an image, rather than to respond to the substance of the issues. This sort of confusion makes future controversies more difficult to solve, because no guidance is likely to be developed from the original controversy. Furthermore, such confusion suggests to the members of the institution that future controversies may be similarly handled, and rational discourse again may be given second place to image-making and image-maintaining.

During the *Go Ask Alice* controversy, various members of the institution accepted or rejected the images to varying degrees. At one extreme was the high school assistant principal who so thoroughly accepted the superintendent's "leader image" that he went into a high school library and hid the controversial novel behind other books. This same assistant principal threatened a librarian with a reprimand when she refused to remove from her office wall a poster that said, "I read banned books." Although the poster was in not in the area of the library where students worked, the assistant principal argued that such a poster was "a slap in the face" for the superintendent.

The kindest interpretation of this assistant principal's actions is that he was acting to support the "leader image" of his direct superior. A less benevolent interpretation is that the assistant principal was emulating the superintendent's autocratic paternalism. The inference to be drawn from this latter interpretation is that members of the institution with similar (albeit lesser) power also are able to create and maintain an image at the sacrifice of honest, rational discourse. Therefore, one result of image-making and image-maintaining is that such actions may ripple through the institutional hierarchy, thereby compounding the original problem.

New Latent Rules

Viewing the *Go Ask Alice* controversy in image terms leads the observer to recognize that a new set of latent rules was developed that adds to the existing rules. The participants in the *Go Ask Alice* controversy thought that they were attempting to answer the basic questions of what students should read and who should make those decisions. But no substantial answers were developed for those two questions. The "solution" of the book protest "problem" alludes to those questions, but its real focus is elsewhere. Thus a new latent rule is that imagery is more important than substance. Furthermore, this latent rule is more powerful than the manifest rules of policies and procedures, which are secondary considerations to be tempered in their application according to how well or poorly they maintain the overriding images.

Postman's assertion about reframing our epistemologies seems to be correct. A second latent rule seems to be that when the debate is focused on imagery, only shallow resolutions will be developed, because it is extremely difficult to unravel all the implications of an image. While the director tried to unravel the images and focus on the processes dictated by law and school policies, he ultimately developed a resolution that supported the images developed by the parent and the superintendent. In order to support these images, the director had to ignore information provided by the review committee, the teacher, the teacher's principal, and the reading specialist. By ignoring this information, the director missed an opportunity to probe for the answers to the basic, rational questions that should have been at the heart of the controversy.

Clearly, a third latent rule that developed centers on image and counter-image. From the institutional standpoint, as interpreted from the superintendent's actions, the most effective way to counter the powerful "parent image" was not to respond with rational discourse or reference to legal or policy guidelines, but rather to create an equally powerful "leader image." Thus the latent rule is image versus image, which sacrifices substance and, consequently, any reasonable hope for a substantial and sustainable resolution. This neutralizing of an image battle is merely "of the moment"; it provides little, if any, guidance for future controversies. Indeed, the long-term effect of such a spontaneous, image-centered resolution may be detrimental to resolving future controversies.

Finally, a fourth latent rule defines the institutional power structure in terms of image-making: Those who can create an image are more powerful than those who merely maintain the image or who work outside the image to invoke rational discourse. The "leader image" of the superintendent was immediately supported by the board of education president. That image was maintained by the director and various other administrators. Those who worked toward legal and policy-based solutions were largely powerless.

However, an implicit consequence in this latent rule is that those who usurp power by creating imagery risk reprisals. The parent, who also was a member of the institution, risked his professional credibility and status by creating a "parent image" that the superintendent felt forced to counter with his "leader image." As a member of the institution at a lower level of the hierarchy than the superintendent, the parent usurped the image-making power of those above him and thus risked their ire. The parent's image-making also placed him outside his peer group, which further risked reprisals from fellow teachers who saw his action as diminishing their professional credibility.

The heart of this final latent rule is control. The image-maker at the highest level of the institutional hierarchy maintains the image by controlling the actions of the subordinates. This aspect is demonstrated in the action of telling the teacher not to discuss the controversy with the students, parents, or the media. In terms of controlling image-making, this directive kept the teacher from developing a third image that would further confound the issue. By following orders, the teacher became the scapegoat for the controversy.

In a recent PBS television series, "The Public Mind: Image and Reality, Consuming Images," commentator Bill Moyers said:

> Once upon a time the idea of concerned citizen embodied the notion of free men and women thinking and acting for ourselves and taking part together in the civic life of our nation. But, for millions and millions of Americans today,

representative democracy is nothing but the representation of democracy. Politics ends with consuming images. . . . In the marketplace as in politics our basic right as consumers has become the right to pick a product from an endless stream of pre-fabricated images.

If Moyers is correct that our image-based epistemology has made us a nation of consumers rather than concerned citizens, then perhaps educators can better understand the barrage of criticism aimed at the public schools in a new way. Consumers want choices. Consumers want low prices. Consumers demand things from the marketplace and are unhappy when they cannot get what they want.

The essential problem is that often the images in public education are flatly wrong. Here's only one example: Robert Huelskamp of the Strategic Studies Center, Sandia National Laboratories, led a group research effort to evaluate the performance of the U.S. education system. The importance of this study (popularly known as "The Sandia Report") is that it reported facts about education that contradict many of the images used by politicians to call for reforms. For example, Huelskamp told the committee that, contrary to popular belief, American schools retain students until graduation at higher rates than schools in any other country. And, regarding standardized tests, he reported:

> We also discovered that the much publicized "decline" in average SAT scores misrepresents the true story about student SAT performance. Although it is true that the average SAT score has declined since the 1960's, the reason for the decline is not decreasing student performance. We found that the reason for the decline arises from the fact that more students in the bottom half of the class are taking the SAT today than in years past. (Huelskamp 1993, p. 719)

Book controversies are a small part of this new public consumerism; but like reform efforts in general, they point up a public perception that something is wrong in education and changes are needed. However, basing reform on the resolution of controversial issues may well lead education in directions that are counter-productive, even contradictory.

Learning the Lessons

Postman, Moyers, and others provide provocative perspectives that inform the discourse that might (and should) take place generally and as a result specifically of controversies such as the *Go Ask Alice* book protest. Drawing on this case, I would suggest four major implications for further consideration.

First, when educators react more to images than to questions of substance, the answers to those questions may be superficial or illogical.

Second, because of the influence of image-based epistemology, our culture has come to expect simple answers to complicated questions. Pandering to the images in this book protest led the school board president to say, without need of further information about *Go Ask Alice* or its use, that he was "surprised, shocked, dismayed, and disappointed" about the use of the novel. He apparently was not concerned about following district policies or interviewing district personnel. For the board president, it was a simple matter; he said, "That type of book shouldn't be on the shelves of a library, especially at that level."

Third, in an image-based culture, not only do we expect that complicated issues can be made simple, but also we expect that complicated issues must have simple solutions. The superintendent told the *Newport Press* that the offending book would be pulled from the shelves. His action was summary and unilateral — in a word, simple. It also was wrong in that it contradicted established laws and policies and ignored rational procedures that might have produced a more reasoned and lasting resolution of the controversy.

Fourth, when resolving a complicated issue, such as a book controversy, is misidentified as being a simple process, the inability to fulfill the expectations of simplicity is a form of failure. As the director tried to unravel the controversy, he found himself in a dilemma. In this case, the dilemma was that the reality of having to act on a solution conflicted with the image that such a solution would be simple. If he shifted the substance of the controversy into a thorough discussion of policies, then he risked being accused of unnecessarily complicating the issue. If he supported the superintendent's action of pulling the book, then he would find himself negating policies. So, he avoided supporting either position entirely by deciding that the book did not meet the criteria for the reading program at that grade level. The book was removed, and some policies were implemented. But the basic questions — What should students read? Who should decide? — went unanswered.

Conclusion

Anatomy of a Book Controversy describes a special type of book controversy. This controversy is special because it was resolved within the institution, unlike those that are better-known because they were resolved in the courts. I would suggest, however, that many book controversies that are resolved within institutions have similar characteristics. One similarity is that the nature of the controversy will tend to be difficult to define. Parents, teachers, and administrators invariably offer differing perspectives of the nature of the controversy. Thus developing a consensus on how such a problem should be solved will be difficult unless a consensus first is reached on the nature of the problem.

Another likely similarity will be in the procedures used to resolve the controversy. While book controversies may begin as matters of substance, their resolutions often focus on procedures. Thus, because the issues of substance are not resolved, the problems are likely to recur; and the effort to achieve resolution will have to be repeated. Repetition entrenches both productive and unproductive procedures, so that the procedures may take on an importance of their own and become ritualistic.

Yet another similarity may be that after hours of work by committees and interested individuals, the final decision regarding the use of the book in question (and perhaps similar books) will be decided by one or two individuals, those most powerful members of the institution. In any institution, some members have greater power to make and enforce decisions than others who may merely offer advice or suggestions. Those who are empowered to solve problems also have the power to define the problems. Definition, in turn, controls or shapes solutions.

This last point is a useful perspective for examining school reform. In the large view, defining what should be reformed dictates to a significant degree the nature of the reform. Advocates of various reform measures may address their proposals in terms of their perception of the district's (or a school's or a program's) shortcomings. But unless those who are empowered to make decisions and institute change hold the same perceptions, the reformers' proposals — however well-suited and rational — may not be enacted. Reform may well depend on how one or two institutional leaders define the problem and frame a solution.

Successful reformers must understand which manifest policies are ritualistic and which are truly matters of substance. While both types of policies are important, each type presents the reformer with a different sort of problem. Those that include matters of substance seem to have philosophical support and those that are ritualistic seem to be supported by tradition or the idea that "we have always done it that way." Failure to distinguish between matters of substance and matters of tradition will undermine reform initiatives because the reformer will be prone to address the issues incorrectly.

Furthermore, addressing the latent policies of an institution is a critical aspect of implementing effective institutional changes. Reformers must be able to describe the latent polices in effect in the institution. Latent policies reveal how the various gaps or inconsistencies in manifest policies are filled or resolved. Latent policies also reveal how the members of the institution work with one another; they reveal the subtle expectations of the members of the institution.

The contrast in the significance of manifest results versus latent results is evident in the *Go Ask Alice* controversy. For example, this study demonstrates that the school district as an institution was reluctant to make manifest changes. The most significant manifest result of the *Go Ask Alice* controversy was that the novel was not going to be used in the seventh-grade reading classes. In other respects, the teacher was not punished for assigning the book; the superintendent was not punished for ignoring the school policies; and the parent was satisfied with the removal of the book. No new philosophical stances about the nature of the student, the nature of the reading program, or the use of reading materials were developed.

By contrast, the latent results were numerous. Not only has the book not been used in the seventh-grade reading program, it has not been used in any program at any level since the controversy. While the teacher was not punished for using the book, some of her colleagues were critical of her actions. The parent was lauded by those in the community who supported his protest and snubbed by his fellow workers, who were upset at the means by which he made it. Additionally, several observers have suggested that, subsequent to this book protest, teachers have avoided using other books that might cause another controversy. In fact, other potentially controversial books may have been quietly removed from use.

In summary, I would suggest that book controversies that are resolved within the institution in the manner of this book protest result in *de facto* censorship. Such pervasive self-censorship probably was an intended — at least, hoped for — result by some participants.

Controversy in institutional settings almost always is perceived to be negative. School districts are no exception. And it does not matter whether that message is accurate or inaccurate, intentional or incidental. When the substantial issues of a controversy are not resolved, the effect of the latent messages is to reinforce that negative viewpoint. The lack of resolution of issues of substance, regardless of how the "solution" to the specific "problem" is reached, tends to be harmful to the members of the institution. No closure is reached on important issues. Thus a major ramification is that the controversy will be repeated whenever another book is so challenged.

The negative perception of controversy translates into a strong, overriding latent message: Those who precipitate controversy are at best negligent, perhaps incompetent. Thus the relationships among individuals involved in a controversy are strained. Viewed holistically, these strains are a product of fear. Parents fear that the information children get from reading may harm them. Administrators fear negative public reaction to the school's role in the community. Teachers fear their superiors.

Recommendations

Schools are complex social institutions. Therefore, the problems they encounter need to be understood holistically. Achieving such an understanding will include studying how problems are defined and the procedures used to solve problems. While this concept may seem to be obvious, clearly such understanding often is not achieved in the heated atmosphere of controversy.

Thus, in view of the roles and consequences examined in this study, I believe that the following recommendations are worthwhile:

1. Both latent and manifest dimensions of a problem must be identified. Any in-depth study of an institutional problem, whether an immediate controversy or a long-time concern, must recognize that even the simplest of problems and their potential solutions have both manifest and latent dimensions. Consequently, both of those dimensions must be addressed. Otherwise, efforts to improve, solve problems, or initiate reform will fail.

2. A thorough study of a problem must attend both to the process by which solutions can be achieved and to the substance of the solution. Ignoring either of these two aspects will lead to an incomplete and ultimately unsatisfactory solution.

3. Educators who seek to improve schools must recognize the influence that their epistemologies have on defining issues. Problems and their solutions must be defined by basic issues of substance, not by the prejudices of individual epistemologies.

4. Education leaders must not be beguiled by the power of images. There are two aspects to this recommendation. First, problems, reform movements, and criticism cannot be allowed to be defined by imagery, because imagery confounds rather than informs. Healthy criticism, reform, and problem solving can be effective only when the substance of a problem is carefully and accurately defined. Confusing substantive issues by the use of power imagery inhibits or prevents thoughtful discussion and the development of thorough, effective solutions.

5. Education leaders must not use power images to disguise problems or as proposed solutions to problems. Instead, they must lead by unraveling misleading images and focusing on the substance of the issues. They must lead by example to promote discussion and encourage members of the institution and people from outside the institution to think carefully and rationally. Thoughtful discussion takes time. Thoughtful discussion may lead to information and solutions that may be unpalatable. Thoughtful discussion may be seen as "foot dragging" by critics who want simple solutions and quick fixes. But thoughtful discussion is the key to lasting resolutions.

Recently, school critics with political and religious agendas frequently have used negative images to portray public schools and educators. These images have a deleterious effect on public education. And, unfortunately, many of these negative images have gone unchallenged. Consequently, real problems in schools often are ignored because educators are busy fighting the brushfires of negative imagery. Problems of substance are poorly defined and remain unsolved. Because these negative images have not been thoroughly and successfully challenged, the experience of schooling, supporting schools, and educating all have been fragmented and seen as competing units, rather than as essential elements of the institution. Most troubling of all, if this negative imagery remains unchallenged, in time, people may accept it as the truth.

These five recommendations provide a starting point for thinking beyond the immediacy of a book controversy to how schools view and solve problems that arise from conflicting philosophies.

REFERENCES

Besag, F., and Nelson, J. *The Foundations of Education: Stasis and Change*. New York: Random House, 1984.

Burress, L. *How Censorship Affects the School and Other Essays*. Racine: Wisconsin Council of Teachers of English, 1984.

Coons, J., and Sugarman, S. *Education by Choice: The Case for Family Control*. Berkeley: University of California Press, 1978.

Donelson, K. "Censorship: Heading Off the Attack." *Educational Horizons* 65 (Summer 1987): 167-70.

Duck, L. *Teaching with Charisma*. Boston: Allyn and Bacon, 1981.

Greenlaw, M. "Children's Books that Have Met the Censor." *Arizona English Bulletin* 17 (February 1975): 181-83.

Greenstone, J., and Peterson, P. "Inquiry and Social Function: Two Views of Educational Practice and Policy." In *Handbook of Teaching and Policy*, edited by L. Schulman and G. Sykes. New York: Longman, 1983.

Huelskamp, R. "Perspectives on Education in America." *Phi Delta Kappan* 74 (May 1993): 718-24.

Moffet, J. *Storm in the Mountains: A Case Study of Censorship, Conflict, and Consciousness*. Carbondale: Southern Illinois University Press, 1988.

Neuman, S. "Rethinking the Censorship Issue." *English Journal* 75 (September 1986): 46-49.

Nilsen, A. "The House that Alice Built." *School Library Journal* 26 (October 1979): 109-12.

Peshkin, A. *God's Choice*. Chicago: University of Chicago Press, 1986.

Postman, N. *Amusing Ourselves to Death: Public Discourse in the Age of Show Business*. New York: Viking Penguin, 1985.

Rumsey, J. "Whatever Things Are Pure . . . : A Case for *Go Ask Alice*."
In *Celebrating Censored Books*, edited by N. Karolides and L.
Burress. Racine: Wisconsin Council of Teachers of English, 1985.

Tyack, D. *The One Best System: A History of Urban Education*.
Cambridge: Harvard University Press, 1974.

CASE LAW RELEVANT
TO BOOK CONTROVERSIES

Carey v. *Board of Education of Adams-Arapahoe School District, 28-J, Aurora, Colorado,* 598 F. 2d. 535 (1979).

Fischer v. *Fairbanks North Star Borough School District,* 704 P. 2d. 213 (1985).

Grosser v. *Woollet,* 341, N.E. Reporter, 2nd Series, 356 (1974).

Grove v. *Mead School District No. 354,* 753 F. 2d, 1528 (1984).

Harris v. *Mechanicsville Central School District,* 380 N.E. 2d. 213 (1978).

Hazelwood School District v. *Kuhlmeier,* 607 F. Supp. 1450 (1988).

Keefe v. *Geanakos,* 418 F. Supp. 2d. 359 (1969).

Lindros v. *Governing Board of the Torrance Unified School District,* 510 P. 2d (Calif. 1973) 414 U.S. 1121 (1973).

Mailloux v. *Riley,* 323 F. Supp. 1387 (1971).

Minarcini v. *Strongsville City School District,* 541 F. 2d. 577 (1976).

Mozert v. *Hawkins County Public Schools,* 647 F. Supp. 1194 (1986).

Parducci v. *Rutland,* 316 F. Supp. 352 (1970).

Tinker v. *Des Moines Independent Community School District,* 393 U.S. 503, 506 (1969).

Virgil v. *School Board of Columbia County, Florida,* 862 F. 2d. 1517 (1989).

PRINT RESOURCES
ON CENSORSHIP

Algeo, A., and Zirkel, P. "Court Cases on Teaching Literature in the Secondary Schools." *Educational Horizons* 65 (Summer 1987): 179-83.

American Association of University Women. *Protecting Academic Freedom*. Washington, D.C., 1986.

Bryson, J., and Detty, E. *Censorship of Public School Library and Instructional Materials*. Charlottesville, Va.: Michie, 1982.

Burton, J. "Censorship: Then and Now." *Wisconsin Library Bulletin* 77 (Spring 1981): 14.

Davis, J., ed. *Dealing with Censorship*. Urbana, Ill.: National Council of Teachers of English, 1979.

Glenn, C. "Textbook Controversies: 'A Disaster for Public Schools'?" *Phi Delta Kappan* 68 (February 1987): 451-55.

Giffen, K. "Tracking the Censorship Movement." *Graduate Woman* 80 (September/October 1986): 1-4.

Helm, V. "Book Censorship in the Schools: Conflicting Rights, Conflicting Opinions, Conflicting Courts." *Institute for School Executives* 3 (February 1983): 23-26.

Hole, C. "Yeah, Me Censor: A Response to the Critics." *Top of the News* 40 (Spring 1985): 147-53.

Hurwitz, L. *Historical Dictionary of Censorship in the United States*. Westport, Conn.: Greenwood, 1985.

Jenkinson, E. *The Schoolbook Protest Movement: 40 Questions and Answers*. Bloomington, Ind.: Phi Delta Kappa Educational Foundation, 1986.

Karolides, N., and Burress, L., eds. *Celebrating Censored Books*. Racine: Wisconsin Council of Teachers of English, 1985.

McCarthy, M. *A Delicate Balance: Church, State, and the Schools.*
Bloomington, Ind.: Phi Delta Kappa Educational Foundation, 1983.

Morris, A. "Substantive Constitutional Rights: The First Amendment
and Privacy." In *Legal Issues in Public School Employment*, edited
by J. Beckham and P. Zirkel. Bloomington, Ind.: Phi Delta Kappa
Educational Foundation, 1983.

Nahmod, S. "Artistic Expression and Aesthetic Theory: The Beautiful,
the Sublime, and the First Amendment." *Wisconsin Law Review* 2
(March 1987): 221-63.

National Education Association, Teacher Rights Division. *Inquiry
Report: Kanawha County West Virginia: A Textbook Study in
Cultural Conflict.* Washington, D.C., 1975.

O'Neil, R. *Classrooms in the Crossfire.* Bloomington: Indiana
University Press, 1981.

Patterson, A. *Censorship and Interpretation.* Madison: University of
Wisconsin Press, 1984.

People for the American Way. *Attacks on the Freedom to Learn: A
1985-86 Report.* Washington, D.C., 1986.

Stein, K. "Censoring Science." *Omni* 9 (February 1987): 42-49, 94-99.

Sweet, W. "Schoolbook Controversies." *Editorial Research Reports* 2
(10 September 1982): 675-78.

"Teaching Social Issues in the Classroom." *Arizona English Bulletin* 29
(Fall 1986) entire issue. Includes the following:

Black, J. "Controversy Doesn't Have to Find the Teacher." 58-63.

Hunt, D. "Social Issues in the English Classroom — Here Today,
Here to Stay." 36-41.

McGraw, O. "Reflections on Controversial Topics and Their Place in
the Public Classroom." 32-35.

Molnar, A., and Walling, D. "Teaching Controversial Social Issues:
Personal and Professional Tasks for Teachers of English." 42-49.

Podesta, A., and Macy, C. "The Growing Threat to Quality
Education: How the Censors Are Restricting School Curriculum."
18-25.

Trotten, S. "Addressing Social Issues in the English Classroom." 5-
17.

Tollefson, A. "Censored and Censured: Racine Unified School District
v. Wisconsin Library Association." *School Library Journal* 7 (March
1987): 108-12.

Weiss, S. "Censorship Attempts Grow: Books, Courses Are Targets."
NEA Today 6 (October 1987): 6.

Williams, C. "Studying Challenged Novels: Or How I Beat Senioritis."
English Journal 77 (November 1988): 66-68.

Wynne, E. "The Case for Censorship to Protect the Young." *Issues in
Education* 3 (Winter 1985): 171-84.

ABOUT THE AUTHOR

Wayne Homstad teaches English at North High School in the Sheboygan (Wisconsin) Area School District. He has worked extensively with developing writers and in the teaching of writing. Homstad also serves as an adjunct English faculty member at the University of Wisconsin-Oshkosh and Lakeland College in Sheboygan.

Homstad earned his bachelor's degree at Luther College and his master's degree and doctorate at the University of Wisconsin-Milwaukee. He was a visiting professor of English at Liaoning Normal University in Dalian, the People's Republic of China, in 1985.

DATE DUE